THE WORLD'S MOST
ROMANTIC
DESTINATIONS

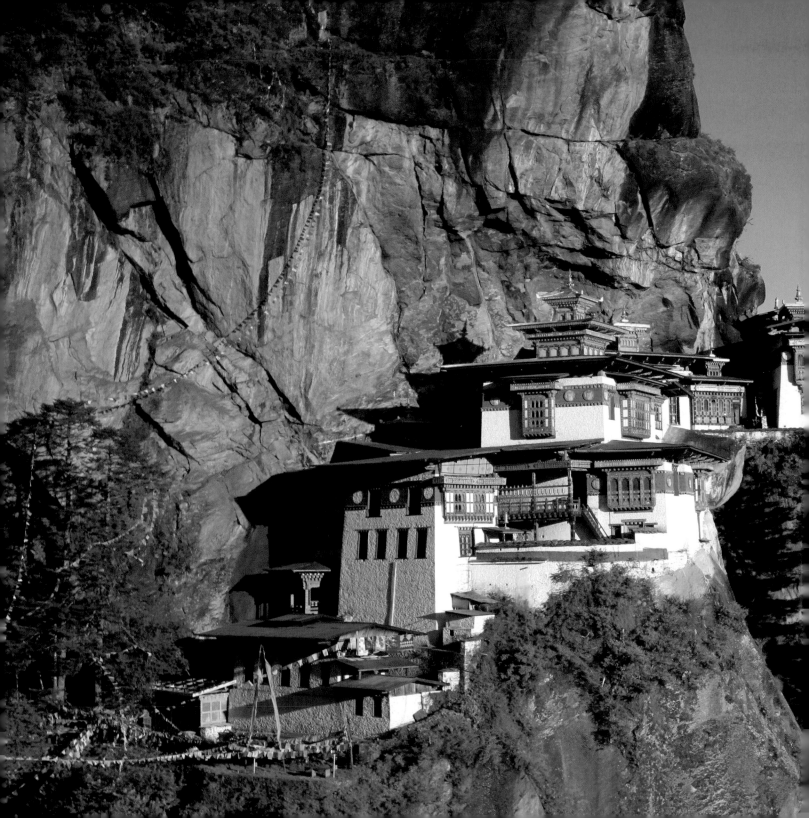

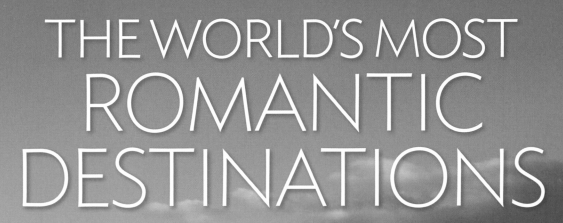

THE WORLD'S MOST
ROMANTIC
DESTINATIONS

50 Dreamy Getaways, Private Retreats, and
Enchanting Places to Celebrate Love

ABBIE KOZOLCHYK

NATIONAL GEOGRAPHIC

WASHINGTON, D.C.

CONTENTS

Page 1: Take in spectacular views of Venice—or go for a dip—from the Gritti Palace Hotel's private rooftop terrace.
Pages 2-3: Bhutan's Tiger Nest Monastery sits on a cliff. *Opposite:* A visit to snowy Sweden includes a high chance of spotting the aurora borealis.

ESCAPE TOGETHER

I've never liked romantic gestures that feel forced. But when it comes to the intoxicating feelings of travel, which closely conjure the earth-shaking feeling of a new great romance, I am a total goner. * I fell in love with travel before I fell in love for the first time. I developed an addiction to the emotional gifts travel gave me—the giddy sense of possibility that comes when your plane lands and your passport is stamped. * I have since experienced all the extreme phases of romance: infatuation, fury, passion, heartbreak, and, finally, an ideal love, which settles in like a great glass of wine. * Traveling the world through each of these phases infuses

each destination with a new and deeper meaning. It's not just experiencing a new place together; it's our nostalgic recollections and inside jokes about the places we stayed, the people we met, the music we heard, the streets we strolled, and the food we ate. Journeys with the one you love are

all about making memories to reflect on for years to come.

This beautiful book, which celebrates romance in travel, is helpfully divided into seasons to spur both practical and inspirational trip planning. Visiting special destinations at just the right time of year amplifies the appeal of the journey itself. Who wouldn't want to stroll the streets of Paris or London in the spring? Embark on a summer adventure to thundering Victoria Falls? Experience the spicy-sweet autumn air in New York's Central Park? Or spend a warm, silky night in the Caribbean?

The best relationships are a dynamic balance of security and risk taking—and there is no better way to experience both than traveling the globe with your partner. Through this book, I hope you are inspired to find that spark—and to wander together in a destination that makes you both feel completely alive.

~ Annie Fitzsimmons
National Geographic's Urban Insider

Left: Stop in to Quinta do Martelo in Azores, Portugal, for tapas. *Opposite:* Samoa's beautiful waters and soft-sand beaches make for good snorkeling and walking.

CELEBRATE LOVE

Romance is in the eye of the beholder. For some couples, a candlelit corner table in Paris is perfection. Others prefer glamping through a distant desert or lounging on a palm-fringed white-sand beach. Perhaps most romantic of all are those who believe that anyplace is conducive to love, as long as you're in the right company. This book is dedicated to all of the couples above—and everyone in between. * In compiling it, we aimed to bring you the best of the world's most romantic destinations. Every continent is represented (except Antarctica), as is a full range of options for proposal stagers, honeymooners, destination wedding seekers,

elopers, vow renewers, babymooners, anniversary commemorators, empty nesters, and other milestone achievers. Are we offering enough fresh takes on old classics (see dancing in the skies over London, page 44) to balance out the surprises we're throwing your way (see cruising the waters off Mozambique, page 104)? We've done our best.

We've also accounted for foodies, adrenaline junkies, art aficionados, music fans, oenophiles, hikers, snorkelers, divers, kayakers, wildlife lovers, poets, dreamers, fantasy literature fans—and countless combinations thereof. If, for example, your idea of the ultimate romantic getaway involves proposing with a bauble that was designed by the jeweler who created "The One Ring" for Peter Jackson's celebrated Tolkien films, we've got you covered (see South Island, New Zealand, pages 200-203). Or maybe your ideal is a medieval chocolate mecca made all the more magical by bell towers and swan-filled canals (see Bruges, pages 56-57). Or perhaps you'd like to walk through the rainbows that proliferate when 445,000 cubic feet of water plunge 360

feet per second into a gorge (see Victoria Falls, pages 86-89).

Whatever your idea of romance, you'll find it reflected in this book. So whether you're embarking on a new love, rekindling your current relationship, or reuniting with an old flame, pore over these pages and imagine the promise of adventures to come. Or better yet, curl up next to your intended travel partner and check out the destinations together. Have a healthy debate about the Caribbean versus Kauai, the South Pacific versus Southeast Asia, or Bhutan versus Bolivia. (These are the best kind of lovers' quarrels after all.)

Once you've got your inspiration, start planning. If you want to see the Taj Mahal by the light of a full moon, make sure you have time to secure the coveted tickets. Or if your goal is to samba through the streets of Rio during Carnival, book your stay before the rooms sell out. Even if the escape in question is many months away, you'll savor the anticipation—a kind of romance unto itself.

So sit back, relax, and get ready to plan the trip of a lifetime!

In the Old Town Square of Prague you'll easily find romance as you stroll between the ornate Council House and Týn Church.

A sunset view of the colorful village
of Manarola in the Cinque Terre, Italy

SPRING

PARIS

Secret Gardens, Riverside Strolls, and Romantic Pilgrimages

Not for nothing has every crooner from Louis Armstrong to Dean Martin recorded "April in Paris." If romance is your stock-in-trade, then springtime in the City of Love is your iconographic gold mine. To borrow from the lyrics: Chestnuts blossoming. Picnics proliferating. Hearts singing. What love-struck listener *wouldn't* buy in? * But however seductive these pleasures are in song, they're even more so in person. To see for yourselves, make your way to the banks of the Seine—perfect for strolling and cycling at this time of year. Or to Le Marais —a chic Right Bank neighborhood filled with narrow, winding lanes, secret blooming gardens, and swanky shops. Or to the Bois de Boulogne, a former royal playground turned public park, complete with a château,

lake, and—from spring until fall—rowboats. But the height of Parisian bliss may well be Montmartre. This hilltop district is home to both a spiritual pilgrimage site (Sacré-Coeur, where the city views alone are a religious experience) and a secular one: the Wall of I Love Yous, which illustrates the three most important words in 250 languages. And in a way, this expanse of black tile is the perfect distillation of Paris: Visit one little corner of the city for an entire world of romance.

Top left: Paris's bridges offer plenty of cover for a stolen kiss. *Top middle:* Flower stalls line Marché des Enfants Rouges, Paris's oldest covered market. *Top right:* Enjoy breakfast in bed with room service in the Presidential Suite at the Royal Monceau hotel.

Take in a sunset view of the Seine, with beautiful bridges and the Eiffel Tower as a breathtaking background.

PLAN YOUR TRIP

STAY • Le Royal Monceau, where first impressions—a lantern-flanked scarlet glass marquise, followed by a floor-to-ceiling flower installation in the lobby—aren't remotely deceiving. Passion pervades this place, down to the guitar you'll find in your soundproof room should either of you feel the sudden need to serenade. Even the hotel's sweets—overseen by Pierre Hermé, France's so-called Picasso of Pastry—inspire ardor. In fact, the whole sybaritic sanctuary vibe is so artfully crafted you'll be surprised to emerge and find you're just steps off the Champs-Élysées. *leroyalmonceau.com*

EAT • 1728, named for the year in which Louis XV's military architect built the house that eventually became the Marquis de Lafayette's final residence. Among the building's dimly lit and storied salons, which have hosted everyone from Bolívar to Stendhal, you'll find a gorgeous jumble of period art and furniture, plus a French-Asian menu that continues to lure in-the-know heads of state and *artistes*. *restaurant-1728.com*

PLAY • Grab bikes from the Royal Monceau's fleet—or rent some from a Vélib' bike-share terminal—and ride along the Seine from the Eiffel Tower to Notre Dame. Or along the leafy Canal St-Martin, where the famed swing bridges and houseboats look extra romantic by night. Prefer a guide? Try Fat Tire Bike Tours. *paris.fattirebiketours.com*

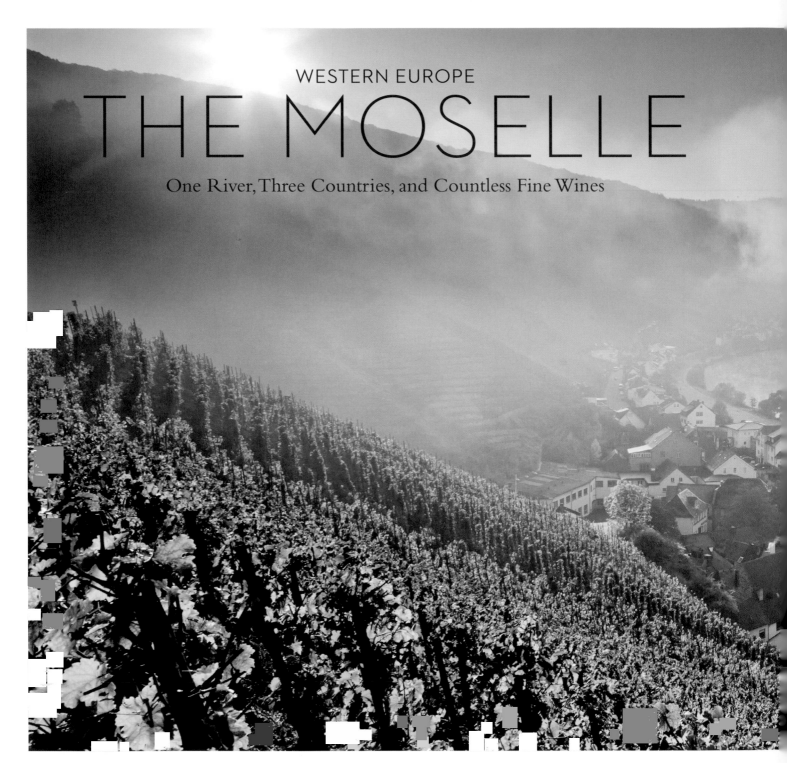

THE MOSELLE

One River, Three Countries, and Countless Fine Wines

The Moselle River Valley can be taken in from one of the area's many hillside vineyards.

As any empire worth its weight in wine casks knows, you can't very well set up a remote garrison without providing good local vino. Thus were the Roman vineyards born—two or so millennia ago—on the vaporous, vertiginous banks of the river that changes names with each country it snakes through: the Mosel (in Germany), Musel (Luxembourg), and Moselle (France). ✳ Since those early Roman Empire days, there's been almost uninterrupted viticulture here—whether by medieval monks or 21st-century Riesling producers—so wine tasting is the traditional must-do for visitors. But the past few years have seen the rise of a second big pursuit,

especially in spring: the great outdoors. There are canoes to row from village to village, kayaks to paddle through the river's wilder stretches, and—for the most rugged of romantics—a 227-mile trail to hike: the Moselsteig.

This recently inaugurated trek, spanning the entire German side of the river and connecting the greatest local tourism hits, is broken into 24 legs, the shortest of which you can easily do in a day. And you really can't make a bad choice: Almost anywhere you go, the steep, terraced banks yield amazing views.

To get a taste, try the seven-mile stretch between Neef and Ediger-Eller, where the trail goes from literally to

Wine tasting is a must-do along the Moselle, especially when vineyard views include the Victor's Residenz-Hotel Schloss Berg, a converted castle.

figuratively breathtaking. You'll trek through Europe's steepest vineyard, the Bremmer Calmont, to what has to be one of the continent's best views: the sapphire-surfaced Mosel doing a hairpin turn through the green-on-green valley below you.

Another relatively short leg is the eight-mile stretch from Treis-Karden to Moselkern. Here you'll see not only the riverside vision in white that is the Moselle Cathedral (the former Saint Castor's Foundation Church) but also the medieval Burg Eltz castle. Because the latter is hidden away, it withstood the wars that destroyed so many other neighborhood castles and is now something of an architectural folk hero. And it's owned by the 33rd generation of its founding family—not a bad record.

Also on the Moselsteig—but just as easily accessible by train or car—is Germany's oldest town, Trier, which grew out of the old Roman garrison. Among the relics of 2,000-plus years of human history here are Roman baths, a massive city gate and amphitheater, and copious Karl Marx commemorative signage (he was born here).

And if all this ambling through wine country makes you thirsty, remedies abound: There are winery-to-winery bike tours and multiday river cruises that allow you to check out new tasting spots in each port of call. But perhaps dreamiest

Riesling is at its best in the Moselle wine region.

of all is the hot air balloon ride you can take over Luxembourg's stretch of the river, with a generous pour of the region's signature bubbly crémant upon landing.

PLAN YOUR TRIP

STAY • Weinromantikhotel Richtershof (the name tells you all you need to know). But lest you have any doubt, this elegant hotel, located near the banks of the Mosel on the grounds of a 17th-century Mülheim winery, is laser-focused on wine and romance—right down to the champagne breakfast buffet that's included in your stay. Compounding the decadence, the on-site Roman spa offers a private night for two. This two-hour retreat includes treatments by candlelight, champagne, canapés, and desserts. *weinromantikhotel.com*

EAT • Domaine La Forêt, which boasts three dining rooms that overlook a valley in Remich, the so-called pearl of the Luxembourgish Musel. To accompany the award-winning local specialties, such as roasted monkfish with tomatoes and pistou (a pesto-like sauce), there's a wine list with 450 choices. *foret.lu*

PLAY • The region's gorgeous gardens are almost as plentiful as the vines. There are Roman gardens (such as the Gallo-Roman Garden), castle gardens (check out the Jardin des Prairiales au Château de La Grange), and, most apt of all, romantic gardens (the Jardin des Faïenciers is particularly ethereal). And spring is, naturally, prime petal time. SlowMosel, a beloved local tour company, can customize a garden-hopping tour (and, for that matter, any other kind of regional tour you dream up). *slowmosel.de*

MARRAKECH

Twisting Alleys, Fragrant Tagines, Alluring Bazaars, and Hidden Gardens

If, as Ray Bradbury contended, "we travel for romance, we travel for architecture, and we travel to be lost," Marrakech wins the triple crown. At the heart of the fabled Red City—so named for the clay and sandstone walls that glow at day's end as though they're plugged into the setting sun—lies the Medina. Born a millennium ago, this old town has grown into a massive maze that begs to be co-navigated. You'll find and lose yourselves in kaleidoscopic, conjoined courtyards; dusty, serpentine markets; and misty, private hammams.

In fact, nearly every experience in Marrakech blends romance, architecture, and disorientation. But the consummate combination may well be El Bahia. Alternately translated as "the beautiful" or "the radiant," this palace—reputedly named for the favorite wife of the 19th-century vizier who commissioned it—took the country's best craftsmen nearly six years to complete. And if the resident dazzle is any indication, she must have really been something.

Celebrated novelist Edith Wharton was among the first to commend this site to tourists. No stranger to romantic scene setting, she raved about the chiseled plaster, ceramic

---

Top left: Colorful tile work, like that at the Ali Ben Youssef Medersa, adorns the buildings of Marrakech.
Top middle: Learn to make your own monkfish tagine at La Maison Arabe. *Top right:* The Atlas Mountains make a picture-ready backdrop.
Opposite: Yves Saint Laurent's ashes were scattered at the Majorelle Garden.

mosaics, and gilded cedar in *On Morocco,* the first published English-language guidebook to the country. She also waxed rhapsodic about the "arcaded apartments faced with tiles and stucco-work, where, in a languid twilight, the hours drift by to the ceaseless music of the fountains."

But don't get too caught up in that drift, lest you miss another of the Medina's big draws: nightfall at the Jemaa el Fna. This sprawling, open-air market—punctuated by the minaret of the famed Koutoubia Mosque—becomes the best show in town after dark with snake charmers, fortune-tellers, roving musicians, and more. So hold hands, go forth, and join the centuries-long list of travelers to be transported by this spectacle.

Other great places to lose yourselves: the archways and alleys of the souk, where you'll find filigreed baubles, embroidered tunics, pointy-toed slippers, jewel-toned tea sets, conical spice dunes, and—dreamiest of all—local orange blossom oil. Take note: If you buy a bottle in one of the souk's pharmacies, you may well get a gift with purchase: a five-minute neck and shoulder massage.

For a more prolonged break from the bustle, take a calèche—or horse-drawn carriage—from the old city to the new, where you'll find the finest relics of the French colonial era. Head to the *Casablanca*-evoking Grand Café de la Poste for a round of cafés au lait or aperitifs. Then move on to the Jardin Majorelle, the onetime home of Yves Saint Laurent and Pierre Bergé (Laurent's life partner and co-founder of the YSL fashion house), for a Moroccan fantasy: saturated blue buildings, palm-shaded lily ponds, and leafy trellised walkways. And don't miss arguably the most romantic part of all: the tiny, tucked-away gallery that houses YSL's holiday card designs. He created a new version of the card annually for 46 years. But the one-word message on the front remained the same: Love.

Sunset casts a glow on the food stands at Jemaa el Fna Square, a UNESCO World Heritage site.

Opposite: It's not hard to relax in the tranquil spa at the Royal Mansour hotel. *Above:* The hotel's ornate exterior and candlelit walkway

PLAN YOUR TRIP

STAY • The Royal Mansour, where you'll have your own sumptuous *riad* (a traditional Moroccan villa complete with tiled courtyard and fountain). Slightly less traditional: your rooftop plunge pool and deck, which turn out to be some of the most spellbinding spots to take in the nearby muezzins' minaret-casts. The public spaces are also awe inspiring—especially the lobby and its epic, ethereal reflecting pool. *royalmansour.com*

EAT • La Maison Arabe, a rambling riad that houses three restaurants. The most magical is Les Trois Saveurs, its terrace overlooking the lantern-lit garden and pool. Whether you go for the Moroccan, French, or Asian fare, you'll eat absurdly well (sample offering: chicken tagine with sun-dried peaches and argan oil). And because the owners have received so many recipe requests from smitten diners, traditional Moroccan cooking classes are now available as well. *lamaisonarabe.com*

PLAY • Beyond serving as the city's snow-sprinkled backdrop, the Atlas Mountains—with their Berber villages and sprawling estates—make for a dreamy day trip. Stop for refreshments and vast views at Richard Branson's Kasbah Tamadot. *kasbahtamadot.com*

OSA PENINSULA

A Magical Land of Beaches and Rain Forests

The rocky beaches of Corcovado
National Park on Costa Rica's west coast

The two most important words on any trip to Costa Rica: *pura vida*. Translating literally to "pure life"—and figuratively to "life sure is good in this insanely beautiful earthly paradise"—they constitute not only the official national motto, but a greeting, farewell, toast, verbal high five, and general catchphrase. ✱ The main context in which the two of you will use pura vida? In answer to the question of how you're doing—especially once you reach the intersection of tropical rain forest and Pacific coastline that is the Osa Peninsula. Here, amid the scarlet macaws, blue butterflies, emerald vines, and cerulean seas, you'll find that all other words

fail you when the rare human interloper asks, "*Cómo está?*"

And though escapes this idyllic tend to run counter to early morning wake-up calls, make an exception here: The bird action around sunrise is worth getting out of bed for. You'll see chestnut-mandibled toucans; blue-headed, black-hooded, and red-lored parrots; violet-throated turquoise cotingas; and hundreds of other species (the peninsula houses 375, give or take). But if you don't make a sunrise expedition, there's always sunset—another prime birding time.

In between, plenty of other natural beauty awaits. You can hike to and swim through waterfalls on the Carbonera River or rappel down four of them in the Remanso Canyon,

A hike through Costa Rica's rain forests is a must-do, if only for a swim in one of the area's hidden waterfalls.

where the final leg is a 70-foot drop into a rushing river.

At the opposite end of the adrenaline spectrum, but no less breathtaking, is sea star gazing. The peninsula's Golfo Dulce is brimming with these creatures, so low tide turns a simple walk on the beach into a sea star safari.

To get as close to the *golfo's* other famed residents (among them, rays and sharks), you'll need to jump in the water. Not that you'll mind, given its clarity and warmth (85-degree temperatures are the norm here). There are also boats that'll take you to the best spots for dolphin sightings and snorkeling (see **Play**).

Despite the siren call of the water, the treetops beckon too. You are, after all, in the birthplace of recreational zip-lining—so at some point during your stay, gearing up and clipping in is all but mandatory. The Miramar Canopy is a great place to do so: Five lines propel you through almost a mile of primary rain forest.

Switching perspectives on the canopy, spend time wandering the rain forest floor so you can stare up at the four species of monkeys and two species of sloths that call the treetops home. Happily, you'll find that great guided walks abound.

Of course, sometimes the rain forest is better heard than seen—specifically, when you're curled up together inside your netted canopy bed. The local mix of croaking frogs, chirping crickets, buzzing cicadas, and crashing waves has to

The rain forest views from a cabana at Lapa Rios

be one of the planet's most romantic soundtracks. Plus, it goes a long way toward explaining how pura vida became the catchphrase of choice here.

PLAN YOUR TRIP

STAY • Lapa Rios, a National Geographic Unique Lodge, is a series of balconied bungalows on a 1,000-acre private rain forest reserve, where screens and wooden beams stand in for walls, fans and ocean breezes stand in for air-conditioning, and sunrise birdcalls stand in for alarm clocks. So the baseline romance is pretty high, but you can take it up a notch with a private lunch by a waterfall; a couples' treatment in a massage hut that overlooks both the rain forest and the Pacific; or a horseback ride along the beach. *laparios.com*

EAT • Grano de Oro, in the capital city of San José (you'll almost certainly pass through on your way into or out of the country). Housed in a tropical Victorian mansion, the restaurant is the kind of place locals come to for special occasions, thanks to the fairy light–filled courtyard, the house specialties (try the crème brûlée with local organic vanilla), and one of the nation's best wine lists.

PLAY • Glide alongside dolphins as they ride your boat's waves, then indulge in some spectacular snorkeling at a nearby reef. Changing Tide Tours takes you to the best spots for both. *changingtidetours.com*

CHARLESTON

Steeple-Filled Skies, Magnolia-Scented Streets, and Cutting-Edge Food

"You can never completely escape the sensuous, semitropical pull of Charleston," wrote legendary Lowcountry author Pat Conroy. And the moment you catch your first glimpse of palmetto-lined streets and 18th-century architecture, you'll know just what he means. Especially in the spring, when the scent of blooming wisteria, jasmine, camellia, and magnolia fills the air. ✴ Other elements that will get under your skin: the elegant steeples that

punctuate the skyline and bestowed this gracious southern town with its memorable moniker, the Holy City. Then, there's the colorful array of stylish restaurants, galleries, and boutiques, housed in a series of quaint historic buildings. And of course, the 17th-century Magnolia Plantation, just 30 minutes outside the city and one of the oldest public gardens in the United States. Home to floating islands, lazing alligators, and vivid azaleas, it's an unforgettable symbol

of the city's history. Reserve a few hours to stroll the lush, wild gardens and share a kiss under the gardenias. Then, drive back to town for some signature local snacks: benne wafers, glazed pecans, and pralines at the 19th-century City Market or oysters on the half shell at The Ordinary. End the evening with a late-night slice of coconut cake at The Planters Inn, at which point Conroy's words seem prophetic: You'll surely be back for more.

Top left: Historic and brightly colored homes, like this orange facade built in 1770, line the streets of Charleston. *Top middle:* The pineapple fountain in Waterfront Park at dusk *Top right:* At the City Market you can buy handwoven sweetgrass baskets.

Many of the historic homes and most delicious restaurants can be found in the city's French Quarter, seen here at twilight.

PLAN YOUR TRIP

STAY • Planters Inn, a 19th-century market turned 21st-century retreat in the center of the city's historic district. The hotel is filled with romantic touches: a lantern-lit courtyard, a colonnaded piazza, and Baker Historic Charleston Collection furniture (a line that helps fund local architectural preservation). *plantersinn.com*

EAT • The Watch Rooftop Kitchen & Spirits is Charleston's highest restaurant, located atop the historic district's The Restoration. The panoramic, steeple-filled view alone is worth the price of admission, especially at sunset. But the restaurant also offers great new twists on old Lowcountry favorites—hush puppies with house pimento cheese and pepper jelly, for

example—as well as artisanal cocktails. *therestorationhotel.com*

PLAY • View the city from yet another privileged position: aboard a traditional tall ship in the harbor. If you're in town for a full moon, you may want to try two harbor cruises: a Sunset Sail and a Moonlight Sail. *schoonerpride.com*

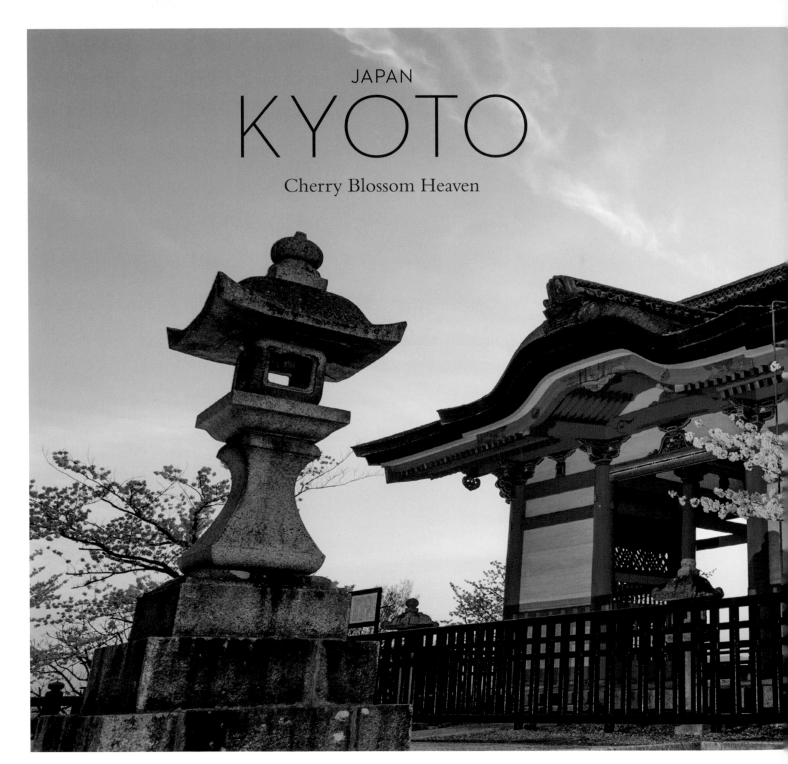

JAPAN

KYOTO

Cherry Blossom Heaven

Cherry blossoms decorate the entrance to Kiyomizu-dera Temple.

Start with a city that's magical under any circumstances (see: temples, teahouses, and the 10,000 tangerine *torii* below). Cover it in floral fairy dust from the end of March through the beginning of April. Then just *try* not to fall under the resulting spell. (Spoiler alert: You're done for.) ❋ The lure of Kyoto's *sakura*, or cherry blossoms, is too powerful to resist. They're everywhere: along canals and footpaths, outside shrines and temples, and in park after park. You may think you're going to visit, say, a museum, but instead you'll find yourselves simply wandering outdoors, lost in a riot of pale pink, fiery fuchsia, and every shade in between. ❋ And Kyoto

is the consummate enabler: Many of its prime petal-peeping spots beg you to linger. Consider the Philosopher's Path, a canalside walkway that's bookended by centuries-old temples and flanked by cherry trees and open-air cafés.

Then there's Gion, famed for its *geiko* and *maiko* (or geisha, to outsiders) and ancient back-alley teahouses. While you should take in the whole scene by night on a lantern-lit tour (see **Play**), by day, you should join everyone and his brother—plus his sister, parents, grandparents, and significant other—for a picnic or pop-up restaurant meal under the cherry blossoms of Maruyama Park. In fact, these spring-saluting sakura parties are so ingrained in Japanese culture that there's a name for the ritual: *hanami*.

Thousands of bright orange *torii* gates line the path to the Fushimi Inari shrine.

For a nighttime variation on the theme, create your own pub crawl or progressive dinner along the buzzing Kiyama-chi dori, a canalside street that's lined with bars, restaurants, and expertly illuminated blossoms.

Of course, non-foodie experiences also abound in Kyoto and are often served with a side of sakura. Ride the Sagano Romantic Train along the cherry blossom–filled Hozugawa Ravine (and before you board, walk the gorgeous green corridor that is the Arashiyama Bamboo Grove). While you're in the neighborhood, you can take a traditional Yakatabune cruise on the cherry blossom–banked Hozu River. Other good options around town? Gawk at the legendary Kinkaku-ji temple, its gold leaf exteriors rivaled only by their pink-petaled periphery, or wander the sprawling gardens of the Heian Jingu shrine.

But if you do nothing else during your time in Kyoto, walk through the celebrated 10,000 torii, or sacred gates, at the Fushimi Inari shrine. Getting enveloped in this orange otherworldliness is one of the city's greatest romantic experiences, and each time you emerge from a series of torii on this two-hour mountainside circuit, a sakura sighting is sure to follow.

Like all other good enchantments, the sakura spell is short-lived. The flowers last only two or three weeks, creating

Cherry blossoms are celebrated on every corner of Kyoto.

off-the-charts demand among travelers (and a serious strain on the local hotel inventory). So act fast once you decide to go; sites such as *japan-guide.com* even include sakura forecasts. And this is one brand of magic you don't want to miss.

PLAN YOUR TRIP

STAY • Suiran, a riverside property that was once an imperial villa, then a Kawasaki family retreat (yes, *those* Kawasakis). Built around a stunning 19th-century dining room from the Kawasaki era, the most romantic guest suites come with gardens, outdoor spring-fed hot tubs—and, in one case, a rogue cherry tree that snuck in under the fence from the park next door. There are also countless cherry blossoms to admire from the hotel's open-air lounge area, where you should try a

candlelit tea ceremony for two. *suirankyoto.com/en*

EAT • Hyotei, on the grounds of the Nanzen-ji Temple, where ethereal garden views accompany a Michelin-starred meal. Established in the 17th century, the restaurant serves local delicacies that include sweetfish grilled with salt as well as some of the world's most beloved soft-boiled eggs (the secret recipe has been passed down through

14 generations of chefs). *hyotei.co.jp/en*

PLAY • Book a private nighttime walking tour of labyrinthine historic Gion, home to Kyoto's most fabled geisha. During the two-hour jaunt past their dormitories, schools, and *ochaya* (teahouses), you may catch a glimpse of the occasional trainee or star as she scurries off to her next engagement in high-rise wooden thong sandals and an impossibly elaborate kimono. *waraido.com*

ITALY
ITALIAN RIVIERA

Quaint Waterfronts, Secluded Abbeys, and Italy's Most Romantic Trek

Portofino is a case study in the power of romance. This once sleepy fishing village first became famous largely because of a ballad: "Love in Portofino," first released by Fred Buscaglione in 1958—and since performed by everyone from Dalida to Andrea Bocelli—instantly lured jet-setters and Hollywood A-listers alike. Early devotees included Elizabeth Taylor, Humphrey Bogart, Lauren Bacall, Eddie Fisher, and Rex Harrison (whose Oscar is said to have wound up in the bay during one particularly famed fete). These days, you're more likely to rub shoulders with such megastars as Rihanna, Beyoncé, Jennifer Lopez, Chris Martin, and Steven Spielberg.

Though each year brings in a fresh crop of bold-faced names, the charm of this tiny Riviera town (population, 500-ish) remains miraculously intact. From the yellow, pink, and ocher fishermen's houses on the harbor to the vista-blessed church of San Giorgio to the Benedictine monastery turned hotel in the hills (see **Stay**), Portofino is filled with era upon era of breathtaking beauty.

The waterfront alone—all tiny trattorias and bobbing boats—is the perfect place to while away an afternoon. But then you'd miss the stellar local walks—for example, the one

---

Top left: Fresh basil is a key ingredient to the region's delicious pesto. *Top middle:* With water views everywhere, you won't have a lack of dockside photo opportunities. *Top right:* Colorful boats line Vernazza harbor in Cinque Terre National Park.
Opposite: Brightly hued homes and restaurants sit in the Portofino harbor.

leading to the beachfront Benedictine abbey of San Fruttuoso. The distance is moderate (around two miles), but you'll want to leave extra time to traverse the rocky coast—and admire the sparkling Mediterranean panorama below.

Another exquisite choice is the half-hour hike from the church of San Giorgio to Portofino's lighthouse. From here, your views will include the Gulf of Rapallo, home to the fabled Cinque Terre (translation: Five Lands), where you should plan to spend at least a few days after Portofino. This collection of isolated villages dates to the seventh century, when the town of Monterosso sprang up (emphasis on up, as you'll see from all the ridge-top construction). A century later, Riomaggiore followed suit—and by the Middle Ages, Vernazza, Corniglia, and Manarola had completed the quintet.

More than a millennium after their founding, the villages remain closed to cars (minus a few early morning supply trucks). So one of the few ways to travel here is via a trail system that teems with foot traffic every summer. Springtime, however, is a different story: Think sunny days and thinner crowds. You can even walk hand in hand along the widest sections—the most fitting of which is the Via dell'Amore (Lover's Lane).

Although you can also get from village to village by boat or train, hiking will give you the most up-close-and-personal views. Literally, because some paths go right past the village residents' front doors. You'll also find architectural cascades that run from the ridges into the ravines; trails that shoot from sea level to cliff-top vineyards and back again; and secluded coves that appear out of nowhere. If you need a moment to digest all this beauty, umbrella-shaded *aperitivo* spots abound. For an extra dose of drama, try La Torre (translation: "the tower") high above Vernazza. There's no better perch from which to toast your own love in Portofino—and on the entire Italian Riviera.

Colorful sea views await outside the executive junior suite at the Belmond Hotel Splendido.

Opposite: The San Fruttuoso monastery is surrounded by greenery. *Above:* Enjoy drinks and snacks with world-class sunset views.

PLAN YOUR TRIP

STAY • Belmond Hotel Splendido, a former Benedictine monastery gone seriously nonmonastic in the forested hills above Portofino. The Dolce Vita Suite, for example, comes with a panoramic view of Portofino Bay, marble baths, your own garden, and complete privacy. And remember that hike to the abbey? Consider going back at night on the Splendido's boat: A dinner for two awaits on the beach. *belmond.com/hotel-splendido -portofino*

EAT • Taverna del Marinaio, on the Portofino waterfront, where the views are rivaled only by the house pesto—a sauce so sublime it draws residents of neighboring towns (no small feat in an entire region that's known for this specialty). *tavernadelmarinaio.com*

PLAY • Visit Portovenere, the so-called Sixth Terra near the other *cinque.* You'll find beauty not only *by* the sea—in the form of tall, spindly houses that date back as far as the 11th century—but *in* the sea. Kayak through the Bay of Poets and Byron's Grotto for the same scenery that inspired Lord Byron, the Shelleys, and others to live, write, and, ahem, free-love here. *wildtrips.net*

HAWAII

KAUAI

A Lushly Landscaped Fantasy Island

Cathedral rocks line the Honopū Valley and beach on the Na Pali Coast.

Carpeted in wall-to-wall emerald, Kauai has rightly been dubbed the Garden Isle. But the island's lesser-known alias is more appropriate for romance seekers: Fantasy Island. Those cliffs you just flipped past, better known as the Na Pali Coast, led the cult TV classic's opening credits. Of course, Kauai is even more fantastical as the backdrop of your own romantic getaway, even without the personal greeting from Mr. Roarke and Tattoo. ✱ In life as on TV, the perfect place to start is Na Pali. Creating a 17-mile pleated skyline along the North Shore, these stunning cliffs have only one sliver of land access: the Kalalau Trail, an 11-mile route that

starts at one beach, crosses five Edenic valleys, and ends at another beach. The hike is challenging, especially in one day, so you can either explore a single section or plan to camp en route. Option 3: Save your strength for a hula lesson and book a boat or plane tour along the coast instead.

Another *Fantasy Island* icon, the forked Wailua Falls and greenery-shrouded plunge pool, is much easier to reach.

Visible from the roadside, the cascade sits at the south end of an equally famous river: This 20-mile stretch—which makes for a dreamy cruise, complete with a fern grotto visit— appeared in Elvis's *Blue Hawaii*.

But the local legend most associated with the King is the now defunct Coco Palms, a once glittering resort. Set in an especially lush corner of Kauai that was once home to actual

Kauai is an island filled with outdoor adventures, including stand-up paddleboarding in Hanalei Bay.

kings, the sprawling property served as the backdrop for the nuptials in *Blue Hawaii*. And the "Hawaiian Wedding Song," which Elvis sang to his onscreen love aboard a chapel-bound canoe, was apparently the serenade that launched a thousand I do's: The resort's wedding business subsequently exploded. Book a tour to view the dreamy lagoons, lush coconut grove, and retro guest rooms. And don't forget to stop by #56, the King's Cottage. You'll swear you see ghosts of dalliances past.

Of course, any proper fantasy island harbors *secret* hideaways as well. As if to prove the point, Kauai provides no signage for Kauapea Beach, aka Secret Beach or, simply, Secrets. Fanning out from the end of a steep, unmarked path between Kalihiwai Bay and Kilauea Point, the expanse is so vast, you'll feel as if you're the only ones here. And often you are. But if you're not, be warned: Unofficially, the beach is clothing optional.

Then again, even the most populated parts of Kauai have a fantasy feel, and Waimea Canyon, the so-called Grand Canyon of the Pacific, is the perfect example. As the nickname implies, tourists flock here, but sharing the place with fellow hikers or drivers does nothing to detract from the otherworldliness of the chasm's waterfall-streaked vermilion walls.

Nor do your fellow Hanalei Bay visitors detract from the town's old-timey charm or misty-mountain magic. In fact, no

Dine with ocean and mountain views at the St. Regis Princeville.

matter where you go on this island, you'll lament the fact that you don't have a camera crew in tow. Such a pity that the most epic episode of *Fantasy Island* will go undocumented for a national audience.

PLAN YOUR TRIP

STAY • St. Regis Princeville, which features a massive, signature infinity pool that overlooks Hanalei Bay. So do many of the tropical-chic guest rooms, as well as the hotel's celebrated champagne-sabering spot (a sunset tradition). You'll also have easy access to the Limahuli Garden and Preserve, whose botanical beauty is magnified by the resplendent backdrop: Makana Mountain and the Pacific. For maximum romance, dine by flickering candlelight and Hawaiian torches during a private outdoor feast,

complete with wine pairings and a four-course personalized menu. Also be sure to book the spa's sumptuous Couples Nanu Ali'i Lavender Ritual, which begins with a lavender honey scrub and ends with a full body massage. *stregisprinceville.com*

EAT • The Beach House, where the view from the outdoor tables is always perfect (you're practically in the water at Poipu Beach). The sunsets are beyond dreamy here, as is the fresh local fare. One

perennial favorite: the sautéed fresh Hawaiian catch with macadamia nut butter. *the-beach-house.com*

PLAY • Pick up a set of wheels at Coconut Coasters Bike Rentals in Kapaa. Then stop into the neighboring Coconut Cup Juice Bar for a freshly squeezed smoothie before heading north along the oceanside bike trail. Keep going for as long as you can stand the lord-have-mercy views. *coconutcoasters.com*

ENGLAND
LONDON

Soar, Sip, and Stride Your Way Through World–Class Culture

With recording studios that produced "I Want to Hold Your Hand" and "Love Me Do" and theaters that premiered *Romeo and Juliet* and *Antony and Cleopatra*, London has given rise to some of the world's most iconic odes to romance. And springtime in this city helps you understand why: Daffodils, rhododendrons, and azaleas set the Royal Parks ablaze. Pleasure punts (wooden boats native to the Thames) dot the river. And every monument takes on a gauzy glow. ❋ For the ultimate overview, celebrate your arrival with a champagne- or wine-tasting twirl on the London Eye. You'll polish off five varietals as you float above the Houses of Parliament,

Big Ben, Buckingham Palace, Westminster Abbey, and more. Next, retreat to the nearby Skylon restaurant, home to equally stunning panoramic skyline and River Thames views, along with delicious modern British fare.

Back on earth, explore as many of London's eight Royal Parks as you can—but at a minimum, stroll the romantic Lovers' Walk and rose garden in Hyde Park. Next, cozy up for an outdoor production at Shakespeare's Globe—and end the evening with martinis at Ian Fleming's beloved Dukes Bar (mythic birthplace of the line "shaken, not stirred").

Top left: Find yourselves hand in hand at Green Park, a Royal Park located in the City of Westminster.
Top middle: Martinis at Dukes Bar inspired Ian Fleming's James Bond. *Top right:* The master bedroom of a suite in the Langham Hotel includes an expansive dressing room and walk-in closet.

You can enjoy a wine or champagne flight while taking in the views from the London Eye.

PLAN YOUR TRIP

STAY • The West End's Langham, London's first grand hotel and yet another mythic birthplace—in this case, of afternoon tea. The resident Palm Court has been plying locals and visiting dignitaries with copious cuppas and multitiered treat trays since Victorian times. Or relax in the Japanese soaking tub for two at the hotel's phenomenal Chuan Spa. *langhamhotels.com*

EAT • Kitty Fisher's, a cozy, candlelit underground haunt named for an 18th-century courtesan who has posthumously lured no less than David Cameron and his wife, Samantha, for a date night. Though the menu is always different, previous dishes have included whipped cod's roe with bread and fennel butter and duck with rhubarb, black cabbage, and chervil root. *kittyfishers.com*

PLAY • Go even higher than the London Eye. A venue called the View from the Shard, 800 feet above the city, is perched atop western Europe's tallest building, where you should try the silent disco party: Three different DJs will beam tracks to your headsets, and as long as the two of you can agree on a style, you're in for the boogie night of your lives. *the-shard.com*

SOUTH AFRICA

THE WESTERN CAPE PROVINCE

Wine, Wildlife, and Wondrous Landscapes

On reaching Africa's Cape of Good Hope, the 16th-century explorer Sir Francis Drake proclaimed it "the fairest cape we saw in the whole circumference of the earth." And the region, now known as the Western Cape, has only gotten better. As the Dutch East India Company was setting up here—and looking to fortify its sailors—it planted the vines that would grow into South Africa's most celebrated wine country: the Cape Winelands. The company's headquarters, meanwhile, has grown into one of the planet's most beautiful cities: Cape Town.

The best place to get a literal overview of the area is Table Mountain. Take the cable car to this massive plateau 3,573 feet above sea level, and you'll find dramatic views of the neighboring peaks, Table Bay, and the city center.

In fact, Table Mountain anchors an eponymous national park that's home to several other draws. Some—namely the Twelve Apostles (*following pages*)—you literally can't miss: They line the coast of the Cape Peninsula, their graceful curves slipping into the ocean for miles on end. Other attractions are decidedly smaller—for example, the Boulders Beach penguins, whose taste in colony sites is impeccable. The local aqua inlets, strewn with hunks of ancient granite

Top left: At the top of Signal Hill, you'll be able to take in the entirety of Cape Town. *Top middle:* Grapes grow abundantly well in the Western Cape, making it a prime wine region. *Top right:* A boardwalk winds its way toward the beach in Noordhoek, a village near Cape Town. *Opposite:* Restaurants offer outdoor dining with stunning surroundings.

and edged in gleaming sand, would be worth visiting even if there were no creatures of note here. And the fact that you can also chill out on this beach alongside its tuxedoed tenants makes the experience even more remarkable.

But so is walking the promontories at the extreme southwestern tip of the continent. The Cape of Good Hope and its neighbor, Cape Point, are eminently stroll-able—and both are must-see mixes of windswept cliffs, crashing waves, and cheeky baboons.

Just up the cape, those centuries-old vineyards have become must-see attractions in their own right. And mustsips: The resident varietals are now world-renowned. The earlier you go in the season, the likelier you are to catch the Western Cape's wine harvest festivals, several of which take place in March (remember: you're visiting during the Southern Hemisphere's fall).

Regardless of when you turn up, a good starting point is the Constantia Valley route, just 20 minutes outside Cape Town. Here, you'll find some of the nation's oldest vineyards (and, arguably, best Sauvignon Blancs). Then there's Stellenbosch, home to 150 wine farms—including Rust en Vrede, whose 1993 Merlot was selected by Nelson Mandela for his Nobel banquet. While you could spend days sipping and snacking along the five local sub-routes, don't miss the town of Stellenbosch itself, where the colonial architecture and mountain views make for another kind of heady pairing.

A third stunning wine hub is Franschhoek, whose meaning—"French corner"—is hinted at by the local winery names (Chamonix and Grande Provence, among others). But be warned: The local hop-on, hop-off Wine Tram may soon have you roaming this old Huguenot haunt like a couple of Dutch East India Company sailors. At least you'll have history on your side.

A sunset view of the Twelve Apostles and Camps Bay as seen from on top of Lion's Head

Opposite: The Dutch-style Boschendal Manor at Franschhoek Winery *Above:* The sitting area in one of 17 rooms at the Leeu Estates

PLAN YOUR TRIP

STAY • Leeu Estates, a luxurious new retreat sprawled over three historic wine farms—with a 19th-century manor house for a centerpiece—between Dassenberg Mountain and the Franschhoek River. You'll have vineyard and mountain views, heated marble bathroom flooring, and, if you ask when you're booking, a fireplace. *leeucollection.com*

EAT • The Delaire Graff Restaurant in Stellenbosch where you should make sure to watch the sun set over the vineyards and olive groves, and view the estate's art collection. Then there's the beauty on your table, from the beetroot gazpacho with cucumber ice to the strawberry cheesecake gelato with rose and yogurt meringue. *delaire.co.za*

PLAY • Take an evening horseback ride through vineyards and forests. If you go early enough (March, and possibly into April), join one of Horse About Trails' Magical Moonlight Rides in the foothills of the Witzenberg range. But the company's sunset rides are available throughout the year—and can be booked with a private fireside picnic afterward. *horseabout.co.za*

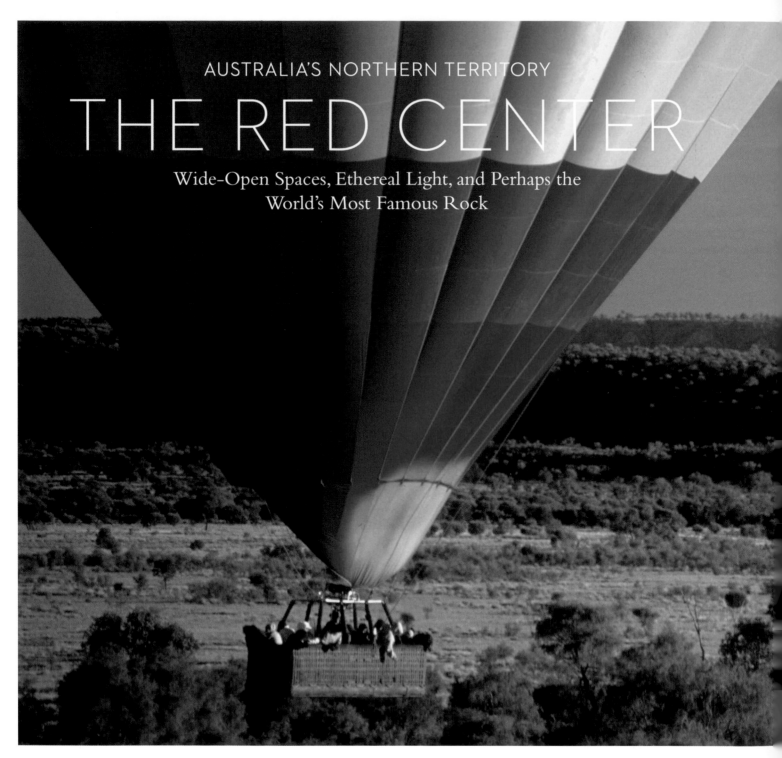

AUSTRALIA'S NORTHERN TERRITORY

THE RED CENTER

Wide-Open Spaces, Ethereal Light, and Perhaps the
World's Most Famous Rock

A hot air balloon soars near Alice Springs in Central Australia.

Dreaminess is in the very DNA of Australia's Red Center (an almost 211,000-square-mile arid expanse at the nation's center). The local creation story, most commonly translated as Dreamtime, describes a long-ago era when Aboriginal ancestral beings are said to have emerged from a featureless earth to begin fashioning a new landscape. And the most iconic result of their work is the gargantuan, glowing Uluru (aka Ayers Rock, below). ✳ In fact, most of what awaits you in the Red Center is believed to have been born of Dreamtime—and genuinely looks the part, from the "many-headed" Kata Tjuta outcropping to the strobe-filled night sky.

(Light pollution is nonexistent thanks to the negligible population density.)

Even the regional hub of Alice Springs barely interrupts the sea of emptiness, as you'll see if you opt for a hot air balloon ride. And you should. Floating over this vast expanse—with only shrubs and vaulting kangaroos to break it up—is the perfect activity for a duo. (Not least, so each of you can confirm for the other that the experience wasn't imagined.)

For an equally surreal but more earthbound activity, try cradling orphaned joeys at the local Kangaroo Sanctuary. Chris "Brolga" Barnes, star of the cult favorite *Kangaroo Dundee* on the National Geographic Channel, runs the place

Uluru, or Ayers Rock, is the heart of Australia's Red Center. It is believed to be some 600 million years old.

and will happily put you to work. You'll each be handed a joey in a sling (a re-creation of mum's pouch) to hold. And be warned: The instant a baby kangaroo gazes up at you and kisses you—*kisses* you!—you'll start to consider the practicalities of marsupial adoption. That it's illegal is probably a good thing, as your next stop isn't especially conducive to carrying small, jumpy creatures.

More or less halfway between "Alice" and Uluru, you'll hit Kings Canyon, where the 500-stair "Heart Attack Hill" serves as your on-ramp to the rim walk. Once you reach the top, you'll enter a world of 1,000-foot sandstone walls, hallucinatory red rock formations, dense palm forests, and one aptly named oasis: the Garden of Eden (a beautiful nook filled with primordial plants and shimmering water holes).

For romance of an entirely different kind, sign up for a Maruku Arts Dot Painting class in the Ayers Rock Town Square. Under the guidance of indigenous artists, you'll learn a few traditional symbols that will let you tell the stories of what led you to each other.

Of course, all of the above is mere prelude to the rock you've both been waiting for: Uluru, the 140-foot-tall, two-mile-long span of (probably) 600-million-year-old sandstone smack in the middle of Australia. Each vantage point and the time of day reshapes—and reshades—the hallowed behemoth,

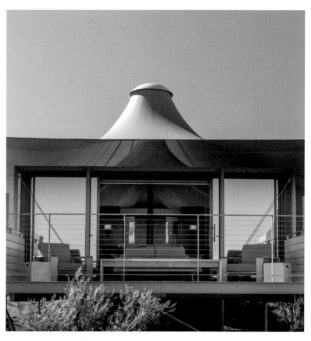

A luxury tent suite at Longitude 131°

to the point that you're pretty sure those ancestral beings are somehow creating new hues of orange, pink, and purple in real time. Or perhaps in a modern reprisal of Dreamtime.

PLAN YOUR TRIP

STAY • Longitude 131°, a secluded National Geographic Unique Lodge in the form of luxury tents that look directly onto Uluru. While couples go for the view alone, the romance doesn't end there. Dune-top dinner for two? Champagne picnic in Kings Canyon? Done and done. But perhaps best of all is the new Sleeping Under the Stars program, whereby your balcony's daybed is covered in a deluxe, double-wide swag (Australian for sleeping roll).

At the foot is an outdoor fireplace, plus a tray of Bailey's, port, cognac, and cookies—the ultimate invitation to cuddle up! *longitude131.com.au*

EAT • Tali Wiru, an open-air feast that begins with champagne, canapés, didgeridoo tunes, and Uluru views at sunset. A four-course dinner (including a legendary twice-baked Gruyère soufflé) under the stars with wine pairings and Aboriginal

storytelling follows. *ayersrockresort.com .au/experiences/detail/tali-wiru*

PLAY • Walking, biking, or helicoptering around Uluru goes without saying. But what shockingly few visitors know about is the rock's sister sacred site. Kata Tjuta, with its 36 "heads" or domes, is just as impressive as Uluru and is a comparatively private experience. Hike into the Walpa Gorge for maximally secluded serenity.

BRUGES

A Medieval Mecca for Chocolate Lovers With Its Own Swan Lake

Bruges is tailor-made for courtship. Chocolates? On every block. Flowers? Copious in the spring. And romantic walks? See the swan-filled Lake of Love, where the local Romeo and Juliet (Stromberg and Minna) live on in lore. Tradition holds that your own love will become eternal by the lake—as long as you kiss on the bridge (an unavoidable occurrence given your surroundings). ✱ Equally unavoidable is the city's chocolate.

If it were simply ubiquitous, you might be able to pass it by. But it's exquisitely delicious to boot. (Fancy a Cuban tobacco leaf–infused truffle or smoked hazelnut chocolate pill? You're in the right place.) In fact, the town has been cocoa-loco since the 17th century, when resident traders first got hold of the stuff. Now, there's a Michelin-anointed shop, the Chocolate Line, among other local favorites such as the Dumon and Guillaume shops.

To help offset all the obligatory tasting, climb the 366 steps up the winding, ever narrowing staircase to the top of the medieval Belfry of Bruges, the onetime home of the city treasury. Here, you'll find a celebrated 47-bell carillon that dates back to the 15th century, along with panoramic views that inspire grand romantic gestures to this day: Many couples have gotten engaged here. You might even want to try it yourselves.

Top left: An ornate wooden lion-shaped door knocker in Bruges *Top middle:* Swans can be spotted paddling through the floral-decorated canals. *Top right:* There's no question that your Bruges souvenir should be a box of local chocolate.

A walk along the canal in old town at dusk will turn the belfry tower and surroundings a breathtaking shade of gold.

PLAN YOUR TRIP

STAY • Relais Bourgondisch Cruyce, twin timbered and gabled houses dating back to the 15th century and overlooking one of the loveliest spots in town: Rosary Quay. For the best views of it peek out the window of a Classic or Classic Superior room. In spite of the vintage of the architecture—and the generous allotment of antiques—the hotel feels anything but stuck in time: The art collection includes originals by Matisse, Klimt, and Botero. *relaisbourgondischcruyce.be*

EAT • Den Gouden Harynck, which has a telltale golden herring above the door and feels surprisingly secluded, despite being in the heart of the museum district. Down a quiet cobblestone lane, you'll spot the ivy-blanketed facade of a 17th-century building that once housed a fish shop of the same name. The intimate dining room, overlooking a lovely garden, serves Michelin-starred local fare. The menu changes seasonally, but past specialties have included

pigeon with green apples, rosemary, and onion fondue and venison noisettes topped with lardo and served with quince puree, mushrooms, and cranberries. *goudenharynck.be/en*

PLAY • Take a canal boat tour. Touristy? A tad, but with such good reason: mile after mile of spectacular medieval architecture. Trips around the canal average 30 minutes and you'll see parts of the city that are visible only by boat.

ATACAMA AND UYUNI

A Window Into Another World

"My love, I wait for you. I wait for you in the harshest desert . . . in every place where there is life, where spring is being born, my love, I wait for you." ✴ When Pablo Neruda wrote his most celebrated collection of love poems, *The Captain's Verses*, his reference to the harshest desert wasn't entirely figurative. The native Chilean spent a lot of time in Atacama, the driest nonpolar place on Earth. And when you see this hauntingly beautiful stretch for yourselves, you'll understand why it figures into his poems. It's utterly otherworldly. ✴ First, there's the Valle de la Luna, a true-to-its-name lunar landscape through which you can hike, bike, and horseback ride.

And the sharply chiseled Valle de la Muerte (the *other* Death Valley), where sunset hikes reveal every imaginable gradation between russet and rosé. Then there's Tulor, the amazingly well-preserved ruins of a settlement that dates back a couple of millennia. To say nothing of Pukará de Quitor, an indigenous 16th-century stone fortress overlooking the San Pedro River Valley.

But the arguable pièce de résistance is the geothermic mecca of El Tatio—the largest geyser field in the Southern Hemisphere and, at almost 14,200 feet above sea level, one

---

Top left: Take a ride through the Atacama Desert on horseback as part of your stay with Hotel Explora Atacama.
Top middle: Chilean flamingos roost in a high-altitude lake. *Top right:* Incahuasi Island near Uyuni is covered in larger-than-life cacti.
Opposite: Mist rises from the El Tatio geysers in the Atacama Desert.

of the highest in the world. Go at sunrise to catch the ghostly plumes of steam that disappear into the brightening sky as the air warms. You can take in the scene from a nearby hot spring if you're willing to brave the early morning chill. Or save the soaking for Puritama, a cascading succession of grass-tufted hot springs inside a canyon oasis. Neruda himself couldn't script prettier proof of life in the harshest desert.

In fact, there's a vast, improbable array of animal life here as well—the flashiest among them being the pink stars of Los Flamencos National Reserve. And beyond the three species of flamingos in this salt flat- and lagoon-filled expanse, there are geese, gulls, condors, eagles, llama-like vicuñas . . . the list goes on.

Not that the area is devoid of human residents. Hit San Pedro de Atacama—the local colonial-era town—for its live Andean music, cafés, bars, and restaurants (see **Eat**). But even a quick stroll around the tree-lined Plaza de Armas does the wilderness-addled brain good, like a digestif after a massive feast.

Or rather, like a palate cleanser between courses. Some of the best is yet to come, starting with the chain of neighborhood volcanoes, where hikers are treated to the most magical views. Good options include Volcán Corona, which offers a panorama of the Andes' volcanic arc; Volcán Lascar, with a crater that's still active; and San Pedro's own Volcán Licancabur, home to the world's highest lagoon, Inca ruins, and a border crossing into Bolivia, where even more drama awaits (see **Play**).

By this point on your trip, you'll have enough material to write your own collection of love poems. And you *do* have this one advantage over Neruda: Neither of you is waiting for the other in the harshest desert. Happily, you're in it together.

In town, visit the stark white adobe church of San Pedro de Atacama.

Opposite: The magical salt flats of Salar de Uyuni at sunrise *Above:* From surrounding cliffs, you can take in Chile's Valle de la Luna (Valley of the Moon).

PLAN YOUR TRIP

STAY • Explora Atacama, part of a hotel group that makes South America's most remote reaches appealing to romance seekers. If you're on a full-day hike, for example, you'll pause midway for a gourmet picnic, complete with fine linens and wines. (And there are more than 40 additional excursion options.) At night, before retreating to your desert-chic digs, stop into the hotel's own observatory to get seriously starry-eyed. *explora.com*

EAT • Ckunna, located in a cozy former school that's more than a century old. Proceed directly to the bonfire area out back for Andean staples with international spins. One favorite is the *pollo a la plancha* (traditionally grilled chicken) with a cognac-cream sauce. *ckunna.cl*

PLAY • Take the multiday trip from San Pedro to Bolivia's Salar de Uyuni, the world's largest salt flat (*opposite*) at more or less 4,000 square miles. This rhapsody in white, all crystalline hexagons, looks like a mirage—as does much of what you'll see along the way (a bright red lagoon, giant cactus forests, and the ancient tomb-strewn Galaxy Cave). You can arrange the rugged journey through private guides and tour companies, but Explora's local glamping trip is the cushiest version. *explora.com/hotels-and-travesias/uyuni-bolivia*

A bungalow terrace at Le Méridien Bora Bora over-looks crystal blue waters.

SUMMER

SCOTLAND

THE HIGHLANDS

Ancient Castles, Fairy Pools, and Other Bewitching Backdrops

The Storr, on the coast of the Isle of Skye, overloooks the Sound of Raasay.

There's something so convincingly magical about the Highlands' shimmering lochs, velvety hills, craggy peaks, and isolated beaches that they've served as backdrops for every blockbuster fantasy from *Harry Potter* to *Outlander*. And much like the protagonists of each, you'll find yourselves time-traveling here, thanks to everything from the centuries-old castles that still dominate much of the landscape and double as some of the best local hotels (see **Stay**) to the kilted athletes who compete in the ancient, summertime Highland Games (see **Play**). ✳ Being in the birthplace of the Loch Ness Monster ("Nessie") doesn't hurt either. The beloved beast's

home—fittingly, 20 miles long and 700 feet deep in parts—sits right outside Inverness, the famed Gateway to the Highlands, so make sure to pay your respects on your way into the region. And for some of the most romantic views of the loch, visit the ruins of the 13th-century Urquhart Castle—right on the shore. Before you leave Inverness, stop by the Achnagairn Estate for at least a drink at the shocking pink bar—if not an overnight stay in the dreamy Happily Ever After castle suite.

Then make sure to ride the Jacobite Steam Train along the same route that the Hogwarts Express travels on-screen. Even the most casual observer of the Harry Potter

Lush greenery, nearby lakes, and a terrace with a view lead the way into the Inverlochy Castle.

phenomenon will recognize the stretch of track that goes over the 21-arch viaduct. But even if you're not Potter fans, the ride is worthwhile. The 84-mile round-trip takes you to places more magical than Hogwarts, including Morar and Nevis, the deepest and perhaps dreamiest lochs in the land.

Next on the agenda: a visit to a couple of the region's iconic distilleries. Good choices include Strathisla (the oldest continually operating distillery in Scotland), Edradour (the smallest and arguably the prettiest in the Highlands), and Talisker (the Isle of Skye's lone distillery, whose whisky is immortalized as "the king of drinks" in *The Scotsman's Return From Abroad*).

But despite such high praise, the Talisker tanks don't harbor the *most* magical liquid on Skye. That distinction goes to the island's Fairy Pools—a series of turquoise-tinged, cascade-fed, mountain-backed swimming holes that attest to the island's immortal residents, one of whom famously captured the heart of a Clan MacLeod scion about 700 years ago. In fact, you can still find the fabled Fairy Flag—a token of her affection—at the family's Dunvegan Castle.

And as you continue your Highlands travels, you'll find you question this story less and less: In the face of such surreal landscape—whether the Trotternish Peninsula's spindly

A sample of whisky is poured at the Bruichladdich Distillery.

Old Man of Storr or mythological-looking pinnacles of Quiraing—you'll have no trouble buying into the local brand of magic, even as a couple of Muggles.

PLAN YOUR TRIP

STAY • Inverlochy Castle, of which Queen Victoria once wrote, "I never saw a lovelier or more romantic spot." And the emerald landscape, punctuated by the tallest mountain in Britain—Ben Nevis—remains almost unchanged since her day. Among the few post-Victorian tweaks: rain showers in the bathrooms, mirror TVs, and a Rolls and driver (on request). *inverlochycastlehotel.com*

EAT • The Mustard Seed, housed in a former 19th-century church in Inverness and filled with exquisite arched windows and soaring ceilings. Whether you eat downstairs by the open-log fireplace, up in the galleries, or outside on the roof terrace, you'll feast on River Ness views and local fusion specialties (think haggis bonbons in a golden panko crumb with aioli). *mustard seedrestaurant.co.uk*

PLAY • Return to William Wallace's day and catch some of the action at the Highland Games, which last all summer. Though they're no longer an inter-clan competition, they do feature plenty of ancient events: bagpiping, Highlands folk dancing, and hammer tossing for starters. Book a day at the games with McKinlay Kidd, and see if you can get Ian Byers to be your guide. *mckinlaykidd.com*

GREECE
THE CYCLADES

Whitewashed Houses, Sun–Splashed Cliffs, and Unforgettable Sunsets

Of the 220 islands that make up this Aegean archipelago—a vision in sapphire and white off the southeast coast of Greece—the one that's almost universally synonymous with romance is Santorini. Draped with bougainvillea and dotted with whitewashed homes that look out over an erupted volcano, this is a place born of lust. * As the story goes, Euphemus the Argonaut dreamed he impregnated a nymph, who in turn promised to make a home for his descendants if he threw a clod of earth into the sea. Convinced the dream was a prophecy of great things, Euphemus proceeded with the dirt toss—and according to legend, up rose Santorini.

With such mythic beginnings and stunning surroundings, the island could easily rest on its laurels. But instead, it delivers a daily bonus that adds to the magic of local life: Sunsets here are widely considered to be among the best in the world. Watch from the village of Oia and bask in the light that turns the cliffside houses from white to gold to fiery red.

You'll want to go early—there will be crowds—to stake out a bar table with a view and settle in with some ouzo and *mezethes* (or meze).

Like most siblings, the islands of the Cyclades are friendly rivals. Mykonos, famed for its windmills (and yes, its partiers), offers up its own epic sunsets—so the only

---

Top left: The Cyclades rival one another as host to the best sunset views. *Top middle:* It's no trouble finding fresh Mediterranean produce and feta cheese on these islands. *Top right:* Ancient ruins of Delos's Cleopatra House *Opposite:* A blue-domed church decorates the coast of Santorini.

sensible thing to do is orchestrate a showdown. Once you've experienced Santorini's opening salvo, take the three-hour ferry ride to Mykonos and hit the tavern-filled Little Venice for the counteroffensive. Again, make sure to go early, scout a waterside table, and nurse drinks and snacks for the afternoon.

Perhaps one reason for the brilliance of these sunsets is their proximity to Delos, mythic birthplace of the Greek god of light. And the remains of the almost 3,000-year-old temple complex that was dedicated to him, Apollo's Sanctuary, are some of the most remarkable structures you'll find among the array of UNESCO-designated ruins on this tiny, uninhabited island, just a 30-minute ferry ride from Mykonos. You'll also find temples dedicated to various other gods—Isis, Dionysus, Poseidon—as well as ancient pilgrimage paths and dazzling mosaics.

Plenty of other Cycladic islands will vie for your attention as well. Naxos, once the seat of a medieval Venetian duchy, is still home to the elegant remains of that era, as you'll see if you hit the Kastro castle complex during the event-packed summer arts festival. The island of Milos, for its part, offers up a natural hot tub of sorts at Paleochori beach, whose underground springs warm the local waters against a backdrop of red and yellow cliffs. And the famously church-dotted Sífnos is also known for its hilltop capital of Apollonía, where the restaurant, bar, and café scene is especially fun. One local stalwart, O Drakakis, has been plying patrons with *rakomelo* (a warm raki, honey, and spice blend) since 1887.

After a few days of island hopping, you'll understand why the Cyclades have been longtime favorites among honeymooners. But until Euphemus tosses a whole new clod of earth into the sea, Santorini remains the setting to end all settings for your big, fat Greek romance.

On Mykonos you'll find plenty of outdoor dining spots to watch the sunset in the Little Venice neighborhood.

Opposite: The sun sets at the Plaka on Milos Island. *Above:* A typical Greek island scene: octopuses hanging on a line outside a restaurant

PLAN YOUR TRIP

STAY • Iconic Santorini, a cave hotel fashioned from former shops and homes that had been carved into the cliff on the island's famed caldera. For the ultimate romantic experience, stay in the Cliff Suite. Tucked away on a private level of the hotel, the spread includes two vista-blessed balconies, a candlelit indoor grotto pool, and an outdoor hot tub that's suspended from the volcanic caldera wall. *iconicsantorini.com*

EAT • Santorini's 1800 restaurant, housed in a 19th-century sea captain's mansion that surveys the island from on high in the village of Oia. Once you've toured the restored rooms, proceed to the incredibly romantic roof garden, where regional specialties such as roasted freshly caught fish and grilled lamb are served with a side of sea, volcano, and caldera views. *oia-1800.com*

PLAY • Make the uphill pilgrimage through the winding paths of Pyrgos—the beautiful village at the very top of Santorini—where you'll find castle ruins, churches, vineyards, and some of the prettiest whitewashed houses on the island. You'll also find dazzling panoramic views and, insiders say, a sunset perch to rival anything in Oia: Franco's, way up inside the old fortress walls. +30 2286 033957

AFRICAN SAFARI

Wide-Open Spaces Where the Wild Things Are

Samburu National Park, Kenya,
glows in the setting sun.

"There is something about safari life," said author Karen Blixen, who gave the world *Out of Africa* (and, consequently, a big-screen romance of Academy Award–winning proportions). You "feel as if you had drunk half a bottle of champagne—bubbling over with heartfelt gratitude for being alive." And you'll know exactly what she meant the first time you see big game in the wild—perhaps a couple of spooning lions a few feet away from your open-sided 4x4. In fact, by the time your guide pops the actual champagne at sunset, that figurative half-bottle Blixen spoke of may already have done the trick.

You can track apes in Kyambura Gorge.

RWANDA AND UGANDA

On Volcanoes Safaris' seven-day Virunga and Kyambura trip, you'll comb some of Africa's lushest lands for the most famous primates on the continent. Starting off in Rwanda, you'll drive through the terraced hills that lead to the Virunga Range, where you'll find ridge-top digs with volcano and lake views so spectacular you'll forget you came to see the animals. That is, until the next day, when you're hiking along forested slopes and someone in your party spots the first gorilla. From your prehike briefing, you'll know to keep a certain distance (after all, you don't want to transmit any germs to these guys)—but only now will you understand the true difficulty of compliance. Especially if there are babies. In their attempt to get you to play, the little ones will dial up the cuteness to simply unfair levels, and you'll have to summon reserve supplies of willpower to back away. You won't want to break the spell, but consolation awaits: You'll soon be off to Uganda's Kyambura Gorge Lodge, your gateway to the so-called Valley of the Apes (read: chimpanzees). *volcanoessafaris.com*

PLAN YOUR TRIP

PLAY Visit a couple of the most interesting Volcanoes-supported community projects in Virunga: the Mwiko Primary School, where you can help the kids practice their English and they can help you practice your Kinyarwanda; and the beehives, where local beekeepers will walk you through the production and harvest of honey.

Luxurious rooms await on safari in Virunga Lodge.

This four-sided deluxe tent
will be home at the Fairmont
Mara Safari Club.

KENYA AND TANZANIA

The Micato 14-day Hemingway Wing Safari, named for one of Africa's most famous fans, begins at Nairobi's celebrated Fairmont Norfolk Hotel (where Ernest himself was a guest). Before decamping for the wilderness, you'll see the inspiration for *Out of Africa:* the onetime estate of Karen Blixen, who, according to Hemingway, should have beaten him to the Nobel. Next up is Samburu National Reserve, better known as lion central. When you're not out looking for the big cats, you'll be listening to them from your riverside tent at Larsens Camp. The soundtrack changes considerably when you reach the Fairmont Mara Safari Club, a luxe lodge nearly encircled by a hippo-filled river. But despite the profusion of animals, the game drives may not even be your favorite part of this stop: If you've come to get married or renew your vows, as couples often do, the Mara wilderness is the likeliest staging ground. Your officiant and guests will be gorgeously bedecked Maasai warriors who'll send you off to yet another epic treat: the Serengeti. In this sea of grass you may catch some of the Great Wildebeest Migration from the wraparound balcony outside your tent at the Serengeti Migration Camp (especially in late summer). The grand finale is Lake Manyara, home to the fabled tree-climbing lions and the Ngorongoro Crater, a volcanic caldera turned wildlife mecca. The only reason you'll be willing to walk away at day's end: the fireplace awaiting you in your cottage at the Manor at Ngorongoro. *micato.com*

PLAN YOUR TRIP

PLAY Tack a Zanzibar extension on to your trip. The old Swahili trading center of Stone Town, famous for its carved wooden doors and spice merchants, pairs perfectly with the island's stunning coastal stretches. Among the best is the cove that harbors Per Aquum Zalu Zanzibar, where you should request a water-facing cabana, a Maasai spa ritual for two—and at least one dinner on the dreamy jetty or in a private cave. *minorhotels.com/en/peraquum/zanzibar*

Cute-as-can-be ring-tailed lemurs walk in a troop down a dirt road—and make for easy spotting in Madagascar.

MADAGASCAR

Whereas most African safaris are quests for the Big Five—lions, leopards, rhinos, elephants, and Cape buffalo—a Malagasy safari has smaller objectives. As in lemurs—weighing in at a few ounces to 20 or so pounds. Over the 10-day course of the Kensington Tours Madagascar Highlights trip, you'll spend morning and night in search of these entertaining creatures, some of which famously sing or dance, or at least appear to. But lemurs won't be the littlest creatures you stalk either. Chameleons are native to Madagascar too; the majority of the planet's species actually make their homes here. Then there's the landscape: the rain forest, the red desert, and the legendary Avenue of the Baobabs (primordial-looking "upside-down" trees that can live for centuries).

Between explorations of all of the above, you'll be retreating to a whole series of lodges and guesthouses, with the best saved for last: Les Dunes D'Ifaty, a thatch-roofed, lushly landscaped complex overlooking the Mozambique Channel and its coral reef. Request a sea view for maximum Malagasy magic. *kensingtontours.com*

PLAN YOUR TRIP

PLAY Enjoy a three-part alfresco evening in the Sandstone Mountains, home to dramatic rock formations that overlook Isalo National Park. After sunset cocktails comes a private feast, followed by stargazing under the especially brilliant local skies. Book the evening through Kensington for one of the most romantic possible add-ons to your itinerary.

NAMIBIA

Standing on the oryx-dotted red giants of Sossusvlei, the tallest sand dunes on Earth, you'd think you have nowhere to go but down. Namibia is so full of superlatives, however, that you'll be spoiled by a whole succession of them, especially on Wilderness Safaris' 10-day Desert Dune Adventure. After exploring said dunes and the night skies over the Kulala Desert Lodge (roof-top sleep-outs are highly encouraged), you'll move onto Swakopmund, where your safari turns seafaring. You'll see Cape fur seals and, with any luck, the extremely shy Heaviside's dolphins. Next, make your way up the shipwreck-littered Skeleton Coast—a stretch so pristine and sought after that there's a cap on the number of annual visitors. The landscape becomes less barren as you head inland; you'll hit a couple of oases and "roaring dunes" (wind here causes the sand particles to rumble) and see all manner of wildlife, including elephants, giraffes, lions, and hyenas. Last stop: the Desert Rhino Camp, where days spent rhino tracking end with an improbably romantic dinner by a fire pit under absurdly starry skies. *wilderness-safaris.com*

PLAN YOUR TRIP

PLAY Add on a trip to Etosha National Park, where the concentration and visibility of the animals around the water holes starts peaking in June. The numbers and varieties of creatures on display, including leopards, cheetahs, and wildebeests, are astounding. Stay at Little Ongava, a luxe hilltop retreat with enviable views—right from your private plunge pool—of the neighborhood water hole. *ongava.com*

Along with animal sightings, you can enjoy large-scale Namib Desert dunes with a sunrise walk.

RUSSIA
ST. PETERSBURG

Historical Romance, Dazzling Architecture, and White Nights

Anna Karenina and Count Vronsky. Pushkin and Natalia Goncharova. Saint Petersburg—the 18th-century jewel of the Neva River—is a veritable breeding ground for storied loves. And yours is up next. ✱ The most epic way to kick things off? Stay out till dawn (or what passes for dawn at this time of year). If you've timed your visit to the fabled White Nights—the period of almost 24-hour daylight between late May and early July—you'll want to celebrate on the street as late as you can. The whole city turns into a party every night, with riverside "beach clubs," booze cruises, and street performances. ✱ Then there's the oddly romantic

activity of bridge spectating. People line the Neva just as the sun is (sort of) setting to watch the 2 a.m. raising of the drawbridges (a daily occurrence during the river's navigable season). Find a spot anywhere you see a crowd on the banks, or take the romance up a notch and watch from the Winter Palace of the Hermitage, a prime vantage (and make-out) point.

Should you manage to wake up later that day, commune with Pushkin and company at the city's most famous bookstore, Dom Knigi. For even more literary romance, visit the Idiot, a beloved bar and restaurant that recalls a Dostoevsky-era abode. And with each new vodka you sample, toast to the thickening plot of your own love story.

Top left: Stop for a picnic or a glass of wine outside the Cathedral of St. Peter and St. Paul. *Top middle:* The grand entrance to the St. Petersburg Hotel Astoria *Top right:* The Grand Palace and Fountains of Peterhof draw millions of visitors every year.

The colorful turrets of the Church of Our Savior on Spilled Blood, built in the 1880s, are reflected in the Griboyedov Canal.

PLAN YOUR TRIP

STAY • Hotel Astoria, a beautifully opulent 1912 landmark and the only hotel that holds private boxes at both the Mariinsky and Mikhailovsky theaters. (You should definitely take advantage of this perk, given the massive arts festival that coincides with the White Nights.) Equally impressive are the hotel's neighbors, which include the Hermitage and the Peter the Great statue. In fact, the latter is a prime posing spot for Russian newlyweds, so if you're on your honeymoon, follow their lead. *roccofortehotels.com*

EAT • L'Europe, where the stunning art nouveau interior sets the perfect stage for live music, especially on Fridays, aka Tchaikovsky Night. And though the Russian and European dishes always dazzle, they're arguably outdazzled by the city's glitterati, who turn out in droves for Sunday's caviar and champagne brunch. *belmond.com/grand-hotel-europe-st-petersburg/restaurants_europe*

PLAY • Take a *raketa*, a sort of water taxi that seems to glide above the water, out to the burbs. Specifically, to Peterhof Palace, the so-called Versailles of Russia, with its expansive, fountain-filled gardens.

ZAMBIA AND ZIMBABWE

VICTORIA FALLS

Walk Through Rainbows

The misty landscape of
Victoria Falls at sunset

When the Zambezi River hits the edge of a serrated mile-wide plateau and nose-dives about 355 feet, the Smoke That Thunders (Mosi-oa-Tunya in Kololo) ensues. Better known to the outside world as Victoria Falls, this roaring vapor machine—which forms a natural border between Zambia and Zimbabwe—is one of the most awesome feats of nature you'll ever see and hear together. ✱ You'll *feel* the falls as well—and not just because the mists alternately drizzle and pour on you when you're close enough. Nyami Nyami, the indigenous river god, has been known to smile upon love. In fact, local women have long hiked down to the Boiling Pot, a whirlpool

below the cataracts, to pray for a blissful union. Even if you don't petition the river god directly, you'll be rewarded with an impossibly romantic interlude here.

In addition to the fact that each twist of the path leads to amazing new views of the falls, this place is rainbow central. Massive rainbows. Tiny rainbows. Double rainbows.

Horizontal rainbows you can see from above. Lunar rainbows you can see during a full moon. Chances are you'll even walk straight through a few.

Factor in the rain forests that spring up along the way and the kaleidoscopic array of resident birds (think trumpeter hornbills and white-backed night herons), and you

The Lookout (*right*) and Hangout (*left*) are two spots where Tongabezi Lodge guests can enjoy views with their meals.

have the perfect recipe for boundless bliss—especially if you visit both sides of the falls. And you should. Though there's endless debate about which country's views are better, the truth is they're all ravishing.

Go too early in the year, however, and several of these vistas will be obscured by staggering volumes of water (or rendered inaccessible). Go too late, and the Zambian side of the falls will slow to a trickle. So your best bet is June, July, and August: the summer-long sweet spot when you can see and do everything imaginable here. And a few unimaginable things too.

Bungee jumping from Victoria Falls Bridge (the one that spans the international border) right into the mist-spewing gorge below? Check. Swinging and zip-lining across that same gorge? Check and check. If you're adrenaline junkies, you couldn't find a more surreal series of fixes.

But there's also a way to live on the edge without actually going over it: Take a boat ride to Livingstone Island, named for the Scottish missionary, doctor, and explorer who introduced the falls to the outside world. This leafy little patch sits on the edge of the plateau that serves as the Zambezi's diving board, and one of the world's most dramatic picnic sites. Looking out onto the rushing water and prismatic mist, you'll understand what Dr. Livingstone reported to

Enjoy cakes and finger sandwiches at Victoria Falls Hotel's high tea.

Queen Victoria, for whom he renamed the falls: "It had never been seen before by European eyes; but scenes so lovely must have been gazed upon by angels in their flight."

PLAN YOUR TRIP

STAY • Tongabezi Lodge, a riverside retreat on the Zambian side of the Zambezi, where the cottages and houses are eco-luxe temples to togetherness: mosquito-netted beds facing the river, private verandas on the water, candlelit baths drawn by the world's most endearing valets, and thick vegetation between you and your closest neighbors (except for the monkeys that live in said vegetation). A lot of the romance happens *in* the river too. Take a sunset cruise past bathing hippos; have a canoe deliver your dinner to a sampan; or propose, get married, or renew your vows at the edge of the falls. The hotel will happily arrange any of the above. *tongabezi.com*

EAT • Stanley's Terrace at Zimbabwe's storied Victoria Falls Hotel, where you'll have views of the border bridge and the cataracts' rainbow-tinged spray. The afternoon tea at this colonial retreat is legend—but so are the signature cocktails. In a nod to the old line "Doctor Livingstone, I presume," one of you should order the "David Livingstone" (a gin, rum, and ginger beer blend) and the other, the tutti frutti "I Presume." *victoriafallshotel.com*

PLAY • See the entire, uninterrupted band of rainbow-filled falls by helicopter—the very view Livingstone described to Queen Victoria. *Batoka Sky, +260 21 3320058*

THE SOUTH PACIFIC

Scattered Across a Vast Expanse of Warm Turquoise,
These Islands Are the Ultimate Castaway Fantasy

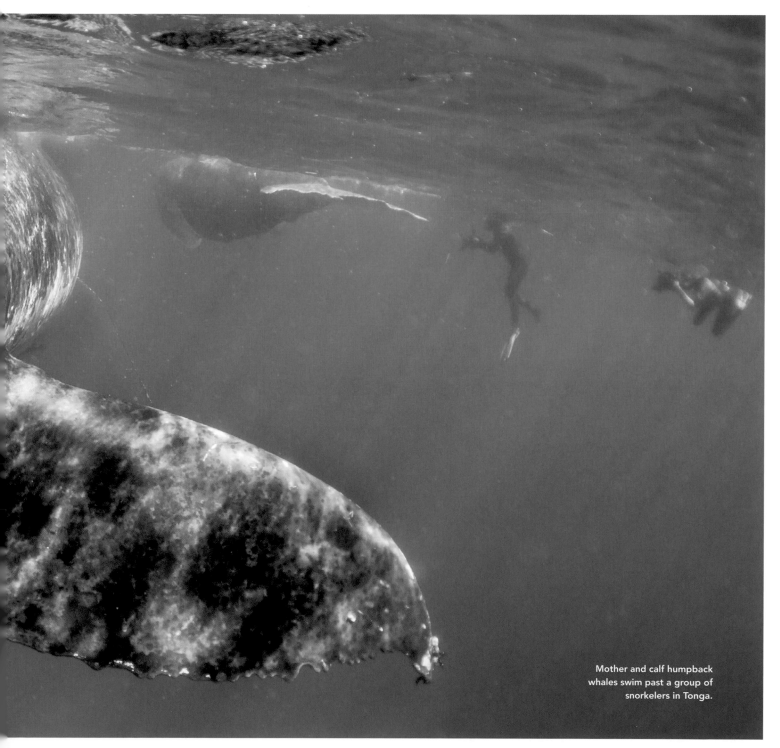

Mother and calf humpback whales swim past a group of snorkelers in Tonga.

Plumeria as hair accessory. Banana leaf as cooking vessel. Pareu as wardrobe staple. Conch shell as PA system. Even the minutiae of Pacific Island life capture the imagination. Little wonder, then, that authors, artists, actors, and romantics-at-large have continually cast themselves away here in search of inspiration. But even if neither of you turns out to be the next Paul Gauguin, Robert Louis Stevenson, or Ida Pfeiffer, your trip to this spectacular and remote part of the planet will be known as a masterpiece for the ages. At least between the two of you.

Tropical flowers are on sale at the Papeete Market in Tahiti.

TAHITI

Both an island unto itself and a catchall term for the Society Islands (which include Bora Bora and Moorea), Tahiti is so idyllic that it should come with a warning: Visitors habitually take leave of their senses—and home lives—here.

This, after all, is the place that inspired Paul Gauguin's abandonment of France, Fletcher Christian's mutiny on the *Bounty*, and Marlon Brando's purchase of a 12-island atoll. But if you're willing to risk staying indefinitely, as they did, the rewards are monumental: beautifully carved and carpeted mountain peaks. Islet after islet encircled by white sands and transparent lagoons. And an infinite supply of palms.

The temptation may be to sit and stare, but if you can break the trance, take a bike ride to experience the circuit of dazzling vistas around Bora Bora. Or don a mask and fins to meet the Technicolor members of the local marine menagerie. You can also explore Papeete's historic public market—a great place to stock up on floral pareus and intoxicating *monoi* (Tahitian gardenia) oil. And finally, board a ferry to Moorea to see what just may be the retirement spot of the Garden of Eden after the Fall of Man.

PLAN YOUR TRIP

STAY Le Méridien Bora Bora, where the overwater bungalows have outsize floor cutouts—key for when you're swimming under your room and blowing kisses through the glass or watching all the tropical fish that travel the thoroughfare underfoot. lemeridien-borabora.com

Bora Bora's main island as seen from Eastern Motu

Sunrise casts the moai into silhouette on Easter Island, with Motu Marotiri Island in the background.

RAPA NUI

Better known as Easter Island, this particularly remote out-post lures travelers with its abundance of rock stars: the 900 or so *moai* likely created to house the spirits of deceased local bigwigs. Little is known about these megaliths, given the shortage of records on the island—a tiny Chilean annex where the population nearly disappeared in the 19th century from disease, war, and other woes. In fact, there's no consensus on the age or size of the statues, many of which are partially buried. What *is* certain, however: They're ancient, massive, and utterly absorbing.

Though the statues are scattered all over the island—generally along the coastline, where they presumably afford protection to their living family members—the most arresting assemblage occupies the grassy crater turned moai quarry of Rano Raraku. Or if you prefer your megaliths with a side of tropical beach, head to Anakena, where you can pick up lunch at one of the stands and enjoy a picnic and a swim in the company of the local moai.

While you'll never tire of those enigmatic stares, the island offers more than its celebrated statues. Take a boat around as much of the churning, iceberg blue coastline as conditions permit, and try to include the gorgeous grottoes and sprawling seabird colonies of the neighboring islets. Also take the time to visit the haunting remains of the Orongo village, which emerge, Hobbit Shire–like, from a grassy volcano. By night, hit the homey Kaimana Inn. The food is great (try the ceviche), and so is the karaoke machine—your ticket to becoming Rapa Nui's two newest rock stars.

PLAN YOUR TRIP

STAY Hotel Hangaroa, an eco-chic retreat inspired by the volcanic village of Orongo. But *your* sod-topped suite, unlike the originals, comes with a soaking tub that's fashioned from native clay, as well as a private sea-view terrace, a choice of fabulous restaurants, and an amazing spa. www.hangaroa.cl/en/hangaroa

An aerial view of the turquoise water and some of the 70 UNESCO World Heritage islands that make up Palau

PALAU

A chain of 250 islands in Micronesia, Palau is home to some of the most otherworldly outposts on Earth. The Lagoon Rock Islands mushroom from the surrounding blue like so many emerald-crusted cloches. So your first order of business should be to kayak or sail around them.

Equally alien (and beautiful) is Jellyfish Lake, where you can commune with the millions of resident (and harmless) jellies. Swimming here is like immersing yourselves in a life-size lava lamp—if lava lamps were filled with warm South Pacific water.

Though you can't scuba dive in the lake—the chemical composition turns unfriendly about 50 feet down—there's amazing diving to be had elsewhere in Palau. The most legendary spots are Blue Corner and Chandelier Cave, where denizens such as the mandarin dragonet (a crazy swirl of lapis, orange, and turquoise) will remind you that you're most definitely not in Kansas anymore.

PLAN YOUR TRIP

STAY Palau Pacific Resort, with ocean-surveying suites, 64 acres of tropical gardens, a sugary expanse of shore, a palm-shaded beach bar, and a stellar dive center. Don't miss the greenery-cloistered spa, where the Pacific serves as the soundtrack to your treatment for two. *palauppr.com*

SAMOA

Huddled under animal skins during a New York winter, Robert Louis Stevenson decided the time was nigh for a South Seas escape. But once you start researching the place where he wound up—an island group reputedly created as a godly annex on Earth—you won't want to wait for a cold snap to go. In fact, you won't want to wait for any particular occasion to go.

You'll simply want to materialize in Samoa, among the blowholes of Alofaaga—rocket-powered seawater plumes that shoot hundreds of feet into the air. Or in the To Sua Trench, a fern-fringed swimming hole filled with liquid turquoise, almost 100 feet belowground. Or on the powdered sugar shores of the island's many palm-flanked lagoons. Or at the last place Stevenson called home: the magical mountainside estate of Vailima, that—just in case you need it—happens to be a beloved betrothal spot.

PLAN YOUR TRIP

STAY Seabreeze Resort, a sanctuary-like spread on a secluded lagoon that's punctuated by a micro-mini island. As the hotel's name suggests, the breezes are sublime here, especially when you're in the double hammock that hangs outside the cliff-top Honeymoon Point House. *seabreezesamoa.com*

You can take a swing over the crystal-clear waters of Virgin Beach Cove on your visit to Samoa.

COASTAL MAINE

Eat Your Way Along a Stunning New England Coastline

Though he grew up on the Maine coast 200 years ago, Henry Wadsworth Longfellow remains one of its most eloquent proponents. The same pleasures he extols in "My Lost Youth"—the "wharves and the slips, and the sea-tides tossing free . . . and the beauty and mystery of the ships, and the magic of the sea"—are still huge draws for romance seekers. The more recent additions of sunset cruises, craft cocktails, and an exploding foodie scene don't hurt either. Indeed, the best way to enjoy the region is to restaurant-hop along the coast. ✷ You're likeliest to touch down in Longfellow's hometown of Portland, a foodie haven on the southern coast.

So make this more than just a landing spot and wander the cobblestone streets and brick sidewalks of the Old Port, a 19th-century harbor that's packed with great new bars and restaurants. Don't miss Eventide Oyster Co., with its inventive twists on old standbys (try the negroni bianco) and, some aficionados say, the best nontraditional lobster roll on the coast (try the version with brown butter vinaigrette).

Another local lure is Casco Bay, home to 140 or so forested islands, several of them served by ferries in summer. Peaks, just 20 minutes by boat from Portland, is a great place to rent bikes and work off whatever you've been feasting on—and work up an appetite for whatever's next.

Top left: Colorful lobster trap buoys adorn the docks at Acadia National Park. *Top middle:* Dining on fresh lobster is a highlight of any visit to Maine. *Top right:* For the views and the waves, take a sunset surf on Higgins Beach. *Opposite:* The Nubble Lighthouse in York, Maine, is a must-see spot.

Head south from Portland, and you'll hit the stately Kennebunks (see **Stay**), where the Bushes, among other dynasties, keep summer homes. Hence the presence of celebrity chefs such as David Turin, who serve up artful chowder shooters alongside the local guys who box up the widely adored fried clams at the Clam Shack.

Go farther south still, and you'll reach the onetime artists' colony of Ogunquit (loose translation: "beautiful place by the sea"). Stop one: Perkins Cove, with its iconic wooden drawbridge and then beloved Barnacle Billy's restaurant, where you should try the rum punch, steamers, and famed Maine lobster. Then go for an after-dinner walk on nearby Marginal Way, a particularly stunning stretch of rocky shoreline.

Your final points south: York, home to the iconic 19th-century Nubble Lighthouse and the nearly as iconic Dunne's Ice Cream (try the Indian pudding flavor)—and the 17th-century town of Kittery, where cocktails at the Wallingford's Anju alone are well worth the trip (try the East By Gimlet).

As for points north of Portland, don't miss Camden. It's gorgeous in its own right, but all the more romantic for its fleet of historic windjammers, their sails billowing offshore, and the century-old Whitehall Inn, home to summer's freshest salads (think purple asparagus with hazelnuts and tarragon vinaigrette).

But the pièce de résistance is Mount Desert Island, where the state's greatest natural assets—rocky coastline, majestic mountains, lush forests, and peaceful ponds—converge in a single national park: Acadia. Don't leave without catching at least one sunset from the resident Cadillac Mountain. At 1,530 feet it's the tallest peak on the North Atlantic seaboard. Of course the sunset at sea level—where you'll also have front row seats to Longfellow's "tides tossing free"—is swoon-worthy. Especially accompanied by cocktails from Northeast Harbor's Asticou Inn.

The coast spreads as far as the eye can see from the rocky top of Cadillac Mountain in Acadia National Park.

Opposite: Take in traditional coastal homes on a stroll. *Above:* The boat harbor at Perkins Cove in Ogunquit

PLAN YOUR TRIP

STAY • The White Barn Grace, a 150-year-old Kennebunk collection of extra-cushy cottages and suites with a full romantic roster: down comforter–topped beds, fireplaces, marble baths with hot tubs, rain showers or steam showers, and—maybe best of all—sumptuously stocked picnic hampers on request. *gracehotels.com*

EAT • Bagaduce Lunch in Penobscot. This charming roadside clam shack, located on a tranquil pond about an hour outside Mount Desert Island, is a Maine fantasy. A rustic walk-up counter serves a sinfully delicious menu of clams, lobster rolls, blueberry pie, and vanilla soft serve. Feast at picnic tables by the water. *207-326-4197*

PLAY • Take a walk around Jordan Pond, one of Acadia's most delightful experiences that is hiding in plain sight. The two-and-a-half-hour ramble follows the shoreline of the park's famous teahouse and provides a close-up view of a variety of natural wonders: hidden beaches, snowy egrets, and dark, cool pine trees that rustle in the breeze.

MOZAMBIQUE

A Tantalizing Escape Where Water Reigns Supreme

The simplest pleasures of this East African escape are perhaps best distilled in Bob Dylan's "Mozambique": "The sunny sky is aqua blue / and all the couples dancing cheek to cheek / it's very nice to stay a week or two / and fall in love, just me and you." ✱ But as delightful as that ocean is by day—and that swaying by night—there are so many more lures here, starting with the dhows. Plying East African waters for centuries, each lateen cutting a gorgeous vertical swoosh against the horizon, these traditional Arab sailboats make for incredibly romantic cruises through Mozambique's Bazaruto and Quirimbas archipelagos, where the Indian Ocean

out-aquas even Dylan's sky. Whether you choose a day trip, sunset sail, or—for maximum magic—a multiday "dhow safari," you'll feel transported in every sense.

The inland magic of Mozambique is no less powerful, especially at Lago Niassa. Known as Lake Malawi on the Malawian side and Lake Nyassa in Tanzania, this African Great Lake is fringed by lush forests and filled with jewel-toned cichlid fish, to the unending amazement of snorkelers. The lake is also dotted with Mozambican eco-refuges that make for idyllic home bases. So if you weren't already in love on arrival, Dylan's right: You will be by the time you leave.

Top left: A fisherman sets sail on his dhow off the coast of Materno Island's Quirimbas National Park. *Top middle:* A woman wears traditional garb. *Top right:* It might be hard to get up from your canopy bed in a Benguerra Island cabana.

Private huts on Benguerra Island offer a cool, shaded retreat while you enjoy the stunning secluded beach.

PLAN YOUR TRIP

STAY • andBeyond on Benguerra Island ensconced in an archipelago that doubles as a national park, thanks to a variety of habitats that countless creatures call home. Just beyond the island's soft-sand beach, you'll find tropical fish, sea turtles, whale sharks, rays, and, most endearing, manatee-like dugongs. Back on land, you can see their collective home from the rim-flow pool at your thatch-roofed *casinha*—or, better yet, from the two-seater swing set

that sits, slightly submerged, in the hotel's bay. *andbeyond.com*

EAT • Casbah Restaurant and Beach Bar at Vilanculos's Casa Cabana Beach. You'll pass through Vilankulo, as locals call it, to get to Benguerra Island, and though you won't find anything fancy here, you'll love this feet-in-the-sand haunt where Mozambique's most renowned catch of *every* day, the prawn, costars with other local

specialties, such as peri peri chicken. Take in the view of the Indian Ocean and the occasional kite surfer or fishing boat. *casacabanabeach.com*

PLAY • Make sure to see the other highlights of Benguerra for maximum local magic: the island's massive dunes, flamingo-filled wetlands, freshwater lakes, and laid-back village life. andBeyond will tailor a tour to your interests.

CANADA

ATLANTIC CANADA

Lighthouses, Puffins, and Other Natural Wonders

The Skyline Trail lookout in
Cape Breton Highlands Park

Though history has seen its share of trade blocs and political blocs, the four small provinces that constitute Atlantic Canada have come up with something altogether original: a romance bloc. Sure, New Brunswick, Prince Edward Island, Nova Scotia, and Newfoundland and Labrador may also have economic and cultural ties. But the alliance's most appealing commonality is seaside splendor. ✱ One of the region's most celebrated features is the 185-mile Cabot Trail on Nova Scotia's Cape Breton. Driving this dramatic, cliff-clinging loop over the course of a few days, you'll arrive at Cape Breton Highlands National Park, home to 26 hiking

trails, many moose and black bear—and one stunning golf course. And if you'd rather see Cape Breton by sea, rent a kayak. You'll find waterfalls and wildlife meccas on an extended tour—or bird-filled marshes on a day tour.

Another regional lure is New Brunswick's Bay of Fundy, where, thanks to wildly varying tides, the most stunning

feature may well be the ocean floor. The Atlantic pulls a regular disappearing act here, leaving the Hopewell Rocks completely exposed. Bearing a faint resemblance to the moai of Easter Island, these massive geologic formations make for a ruggedly romantic backdrop whether you're strolling or sitting down to a meal (see **Eat**).

Sitting on rocky terrain, the window-filled Fogo Island Inn offers endless water views of the Atlantic.

Then there's Prince Edward Island, where the most beautiful nod to nautical life is the profusion of lighthouses: A grand total of 52 in a wide variety of colors, shapes, and sizes punctuates the island's renowned red cliffs. Spend a day lighthouse-hopping, making sure to climb all the way to the top (where you're allowed) for endless ocean views. And if you're feeling that a day of lighthouse exploring isn't enough, spend the night in one, too: Check out the Keeper's Quarters or the Tower Rooms at the West Point Lighthouse Inn.

In Newfoundland and Labrador, the maritime magnificence takes an altogether different form: whales. One great way to see them is to book a boat trip to Witless Bay Ecological Reserve. This group of four rocky islands hosts humpbacks and minkes, which are joined each summer by millions of seabirds, most notably, the members of the largest puffin colony on the continent. Visit by June, if you can, and you'll pass through the so-called Iceberg Alley, where ton upon ton of Arctic bergs that have broken off from Greenlandic glaciers parade by every year.

Elsewhere in Newfoundland and Labrador, make time to visit the small, remote fishing outpost of Fogo Island, where you'll find almost 125 miles' worth of exquisite hiking trails that may or may not have started as caribou and fox

Moose spotting will be a common theme of your visit to Cape Breton.

footpaths. The local lore is that the tracks were etched by lovers who were courting between villages. And here, within the borders of the Romance Bloc, that explanation seems perfectly plausible.

PLAN YOUR TRIP

STAY • Fogo Island Inn, a secluded, striking span of glass and wood on stilts that help minimize the building's footprint. At the same time this National Geographic Unique Lodge maximizes your view of the ocean with floor-to-ceiling windows and an abundance of cozy furniture. When you're not cozying up in the lounge, library, cinema, or rooftop hot tubs, take advantage of the inn's numerous hiking, boating, and biking options. *fogoislandinn.ca*

EAT • "Dining on the Ocean Floor," catered by the Flying Apron Inn & Cookery, is available on set dates throughout the summer, as well as on request (conditions permitting). Awesome for the setting alone—Fundy Bay's naked seabed, 50 feet belowground—the experience also includes a foraging session, a four-course seafood-intensive feast with pairings from a local winery, a bonfire, and a tour of the fossils and tidal pools of Burntcoat Head

Park, scene of the planet's highest recorded tides. *flyingaproncookery.com*

PLAY • Those same crazy tides make for superb rafting on the Shubenacadie River, where the Bay of Fundy's waters are funneled to create a surge. Known as a tidal bore, the front of that surge is what you'll be riding—to your unending amazement. The urge to cling to each other will be strong, but keep paddling. *tidalboreadventures.ca*

THE SOUTH OF
FRANCE

The Landscapes That Inspired Some of the World's Most Beloved Art

Sunflowers and lavender paint the fields of Verdon Park in Provence.

"Like walking into a painting" is an overused phrase—especially in tourism circles. But to understand how eerily accurate it is in the South of France—aka Le Midi—you need only consider the number of artists who have lived, painted, and been immortalized by museums here. The short list includes Marc Chagall, Pablo Picasso, Vincent Van Gogh, Paul Cézanne, Henri Matisse, and Pierre-Auguste Renoir. In fact, so many of their masterpieces include local landmarks that this is the rare place where at every turn, you see something not only magnificent but familiar—even if you've never been here before. ✻ Of course, the very features that make

Stop at Brasserie Les Deux Garçons in Provence for a beer or cocktail.

Le Midi so artistically rich make it romantically rich as well: the magical light, the hidden beaches, the moody mountains, the ancient ruins, the vineyards, and the cliff-top villages. To say nothing of the lavender and sunflower fields, a summer spectacle so awe-inspiring—and so specific to the region—that many travelers come just to see (and smell) the flowers.

But even if you're not looking for a florally focused itinerary, you should plan to arrive in July (early August at the latest) to at least catch a glimpse of Provence's world-famous rhapsody in purple and yellow. Though there's a whole series of Routes de la Lavande (lavender routes), the most iconic fields are located in front of Senanque Abbey, near the towering, golden stone village of Gordes—and in Grasse, the so-called perfume capital of the world. As for sunflowers, make sure to drive by the roadside fields in Arles, where Van Gogh was inspired to paint his vaunted variations on the theme (and, for that matter, "Starry Night"). You'll marvel at how similar the landscape looks today.

PLAN YOUR TRIP

STAY Château Eza, a 400-year-old former princely lair that serves as gorgeous gâteau topper to a layer cake of Riviera romance. Beneath the castle sits Eze, a beautifully preserved medieval town that overlooks the sea. Book a room with a private balcony so you can gorge on views that include St. Tropez and Corsica. *chateaueza.com*

St. Reparate Cathedral is the focal point of Old Nice's plaza.

Along the Côte d'Azur (the French Riviera), hillside towns, ornate bridges, and blue coasts are everyday views.

Another favorite local painting theme: still life with *vin*. Artists here have never had to look far for this particular muse, because Provence is home to no fewer than 20 wine appellations—and in a happy coincidence for summer visitors, some of the most renowned rosés on Earth. The seaside resort town of Bandol is an especially beautiful tasting spot; make sure to try the rosés at Château de Pibaron, a sprawling estate that overlooks the Mediterranean, or Château Sante Anne, near the old stone village of Evenos. Bandol's coastal neighbor, Cassis, is another ideal rosé pilgrimage site, where you'll find the gorgeous, ancient, and arguably revered vineyards of Clos Ste. Magdeleine, whose terraced hills are bordered by 270 miles of protected aqua sea of Parc National des Calanques.

For painterly backdrops of a different kind, visit the region's profusion of celebrated Roman ruins. You'll recognize them from many a masterpiece—but the in-person experience is infinitely more romantic, and one of the best ways to view these ancient artifacts is by water. You can, for example, swim or rent a kayak along the Gardon River so you can float beneath the 2,000-year-old double-decker Pont du Gard aqueduct. Or sit under the stars at the equally ancient Théâtre Antique in Orange, where there are still music performances during the summer. Or climb to the top of the Arles Arena, where the nosebleed seats of yesteryear now make for lovely lookout points and picnic sites.

To see a whole other side of Provence, visit aristocratic Aix, where you'll find a wealth of baroque architecture and inviting public spaces. Everyone's favorite example of the latter is the Cours Mirabeau, a beautiful boulevard lined

PLAN YOUR TRIP

EAT La Vague d'Or, where the Michelin-starred Mediterranean menu pairs beautifully with the views of the Gulf of St. Tropez from your pine-shaded spot on the terrace. Specialties include the turbot poached in seawater, lemongrass, and seaweed. vaguedor.com

A stay in Château Eza's Superior Room includes breathtaking sights you can take in from bed.

with trees, dotted with fountains, and filled with pretty people. It makes for a supremely romantic stroll, but you should also take in the scene from an outdoor table at the 18th-century Les Deux Garçons. You'll be getting the same perspective as the many artists who used to spend time here—from Picasso to Cézanne.

Cézanne, in fact, grew up in Aix and spent years painting in the area. You can visit his studio, Les Lauves, where you'll still find his brushes, palette, and still-life objects. Or, for a touch more romance, visit the mountain that frequently served as his muse: Mont Sainte-Victoire, where you'll find enchanting trails, a 17th-century priory, a tiny cave chapel—and, from the Pic des Mouches, a

view of Provence that stretches all the way to the sea on a clear day.

Ah, *oui*, the sea: the other essential element to summer in the South of France. Right next door to Provence sits the fabled French Riviera, or the Côte d'Azur—another setting

PLAN YOUR TRIP

PLAY Experience island life. Located between Marseilles and Cannes, the Îles d'Hyères (also known as the Îles d'Or because of their rocks' golden glow) feel a world away from the hustle and bustle of the Riviera. Everyone's favorite *île* is little Porquerolles, where you'll find only undeveloped beaches, a 19th-century village, and lots and lots of trees.

you may recognize, whether from Monet's afternoons in Antibes, Matisse's Bay of Nice, or Bonnard's boats of Cannes (humble precursors of the ones that now pull into port for the famous international film festival that takes place here every May).

Though all three of those cities remain must-sees, some of the Riviera's lesser-known spots are equally beautiful and a lot more tranquil: Theoule-sur-mer, a little town with lovely bars and cafés on the water; Villefranche-sur-mer, a beach-blessed old fishing village near Nice; and, for something more chic, Cap Ferrat's Paloma Plage, where the water is so clear you may actually see scuba divers while you float on the surface here.

Or head about 15 minutes inland to St. Paul de Vence, a charming hilltop village where the medieval and the modern blend seamlessly. This ancient town—one of the oldest on the Riviera—is home to the Maeght Foundation's galleries and sculpture garden, among other contemporary art legends. It also offers views of the snowcapped Alps on one side and the Mediterranean on the other.

Back at your Riviera lair (see **Stay**), embrace your own creative spirit and take a stab at sketching each other (like a latter-day Picasso and Gilot). Don't worry. Artistic talent seeps in by osmosis here. And no souvenirs could be more romantic.

The cityscape of Cassis is filled with colorful facades that are reflected in the harbor's waters.

DALMATIAN COAST

Marble Streets, Cerulean Seas, and a Thousand Treasures in Between

As romantic backdrops go, Dalmatia is, quite literally, one for the ages. It's been the scene of everything from *Game of Thrones* weddings to Beyoncé and Jay Z's babymoon (Blue Ivy is reportedly named for a local tree). And summer is the best time to experience this magical place. The transparent turquoise coves have warmed to perfection; all things tasty are in season; and long, languorous days mean bonus hours for taking in the impressive lineup of bays, bluffs, beaches, and cypress forests. ✱ Landing in Dubrovnik, you'll see right away why it's known as Thesaurum Mundi ("treasure of the world")—particularly if you walk the city walls.

First built in the 9th century, they were fortified in the 14th and 15th centuries, eventually reaching heights of more than 80 feet. The upshot for 21st-century visitors: dramatic views of the city itself, with its red roofs and baroque domes, and the adjacent, shimmering Adriatic.

For even more expansive sea and city panoramas, hike or take the cable car up to Dubrovnik's Mount Srd. Where the presence of both a 19th-century fortress and a 21st-century bar-restaurant makes perfect sense: On a clear day, you can see almost 40 miles in any direction.

Top left: Follow this boardwalk in Krka to the Skradinski Buk waterfalls and a swimming hole below. *Top middle:* You won't want for selfie-taking opportunities in the golden city of Dubrovnik. *Top right:* Dine with city views on Villa Orsula's restaurant terrace. *Opposite:* Korcula Island, home to many *Game of Thrones* scenes, is illuminated at sunset.

After spending the day among the city's enchanting sights, from the streets themselves—all gleaming marble and secret passageways—to the cupola of the cathedral, make your way to Buza, one of the most romantic sunset spots on Earth. Also known as the "hole in the wall," this café-bar feels magically suspended along seaside cliffs just outside the Old City's southern wall. Settle in with cold drinks and small snacks and enjoy incomparable views of the Adriatic. Buza also offers access to the diving cliff known locally as "the lion." Even if you don't partake yourself, watching braver souls plunge into the sea is worth the trip.

Of course, Dalmatia's islands beckon as well. The closest include little Lokrum (just 15 minutes away from Dubrovnik by ferry), home to beautiful botanical gardens, a Benedictine monastery, free-range peacocks, a swimmable saltwater lagoon, and—for *Game of Thrones* fans—the familiar landscapes of the fabled city of Qarth. Go farther afield—three hours north by ferry—and you'll find Hvar, where celebrity hangouts brush up against Gothic palaces.

Not far from Hvar is the rising-star isle of Korcula, whose fishing villages, pebble beaches, vineyards, olive groves, and old town (Marco Polo's possible birthplace) make for a perfect day trip. Add a visit to the Konoba Mate, a family farm turned restaurant, and you'll find some of the best takes on traditional Dalmatian fare. Try the Labourers Plate—a local antipasto that overflows with flavorful produce—and the house sage syrup.

Of course, beauty isn't the exclusive domain of the coast. Head inland to Krka National Park, where you'll find the multilevel Skradinski Buk falls and swimming hole—part of a bucolic backdrop you may recognize from season four of *Game of Thrones.* But whether or not you're fans of the series, the Dalmatian landscape will have the same effect: You'll want to hide yourselves away and simply binge-view.

The cobblestone streets and historic buildings make outdoor dining a priority in Dubrovnik, a UNESCO World Heritage site.

Opposite: The Krka cascading falls *Above:* Book the Royal Suite at Villa Orsula in Dubrovnik for this view.

PLAN YOUR TRIP

STAY • Dubrovnik's Villa Orsula, a ravishingly refurbished old aristocratic residence on the Adriatic with seafront gardens, vistas of the Old City center, a private, butlered beach—and the occasional Lannister sighting. This beautiful stone villa just a stone's throw from the island of Lokrum is where many *Game of Thrones* cast members stay while filming. Ask for a suite with sea or harbor views. *adriaticluxuryhotels.com*

EAT • Zori, on an island hideaway just off Hvar, where breathtaking Adriatic views accompany such specialties as the sea bass fillet in *crépinette* (a flattened sausage) with Dalmatian herbs, figs, elderflower, and citrus. Or splurge on the tasting menu, which includes lobster buzzara and tagliatelle with scampi and truffles. *zori.hr*

PLAY • Split, Dalmatia's largest city, is home to a heady blend of urban life and ancient history that begs to be explored. Diocletian's Palace, built by the fourth-century Roman emperor of the same name, should top your list. Once home to thousands, the palace's complex includes more than 200 buildings. And the setting—majestic mountains alongside the aqua Adriatic—can't be beat.

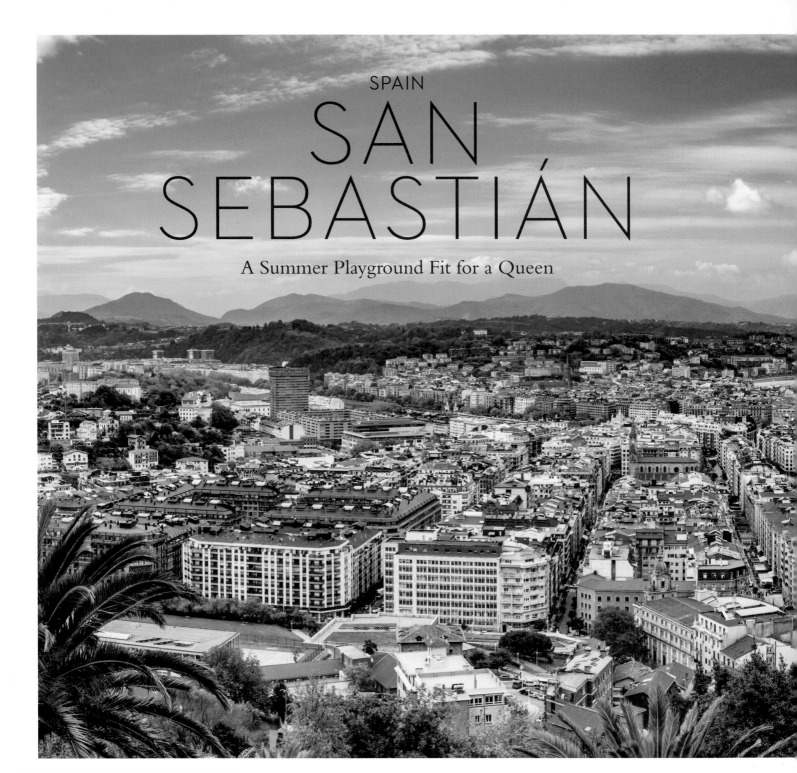

SPAIN

SAN SEBASTIÁN

A Summer Playground Fit for a Queen

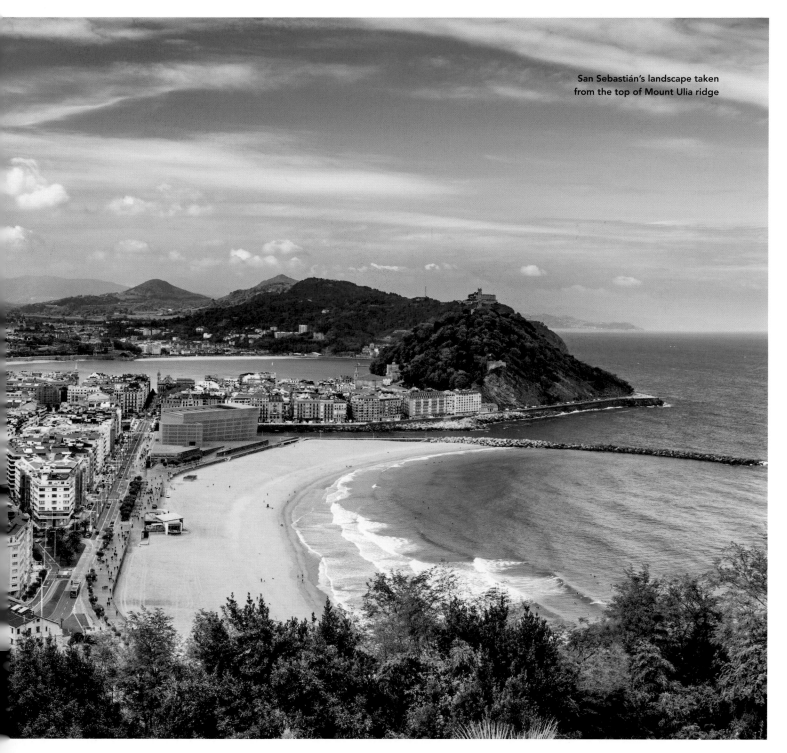

San Sebastián's landscape taken
from the top of Mount Ulia ridge

If royals can be relied upon for one thing, it's exquisite taste in holiday spots. But when Queen Isabel II christened San Sebastián a royal summer retreat almost 125 years ago, she didn't know the half of it. Going only on the perfect beaches and climate, she had no idea that future generations of Spanish aristocracy would be able to eat better in the streets than in the palace. Or that the city would win the coveted European Capital of Culture title. Or that summers here would turn into one grand festival. In other words, you won't live like royalty when you visit this Basque beauty; you'll live even better. ✱ More recent history has seen a culinary

explosion in San Sebastián, now a Michelin star–spangled city where foodies come for the restaurants alone (see **Eat**). The local *pintxos* (a version of tapas) have become equally renowned. And the Parte Vieja neighborhood is now a frequent staging area for *txikiteos*—the Basque term for pintxo crawls. Against a backdrop of 19th-century buildings and

winding cobblestone streets, you can follow prescribed *rutas de pintxos* (tapas trails) or invent your own. Either way, you'll want to hit a few of the places that make all the best-of lists. Try Bar Zeruko, Fuego Negro, and Ganbara— and expect everything from croquettes to the Spanish equivalent of sliders.

Iron-railed promenades offer plenty of spots to stop and take in the sunset over Concha Bay.

Then there are all the upgrades that preceded the city's European Capital of Culture reign. An old tobacco factory, for example, was transformed into the stunning new Tabakalera International Centre for Contemporary Culture, where you'll find a packed calendar of exhibits, performances, workshops, and screenings. After its own renovation, the lovely 16th-century convent that houses the San Telmo Museum has freshly expanded spaces in which to explore the evolution of Basque society.

Not that the local cultural offerings are purely serious—especially once the summer-long series of festivals begins. Enjoy celebrating the theme of the month, whether it's June's Surfilmfestibal (the best in surf cinema), July's International Jazz Festival, or August's Aste Nagusia—a Basque party week with music, dance, and drinks.

For all the changes that have taken place since the days of Queen Isabel II, however, the same features that drew her here are no less seductive. The most famous is the spectacular shell-shaped La Concha beach, also known as the Pearl of the Cantabrian Sea. You could spend hours sampling the area's restaurants and views, but Café de la Concha is the ultimate stop for both. Be sure to take a stroll on the promenade, where the turn-of-the-century railing is an icon unto itself.

Enjoy cuisine San Sebastián style with traditional tapas.

You'll also want to check out the surfing mecca of Zurriola; the sunbathing hot spot of Ondarreta; and the small, secluded Isla Santa Clara beach, where you should go for a dip and a drink—all experiences fit for a royal.

PLAN YOUR TRIP

STAY • Hotel Maria Cristina, the newly renovated belle epoque grande dame. Inaugurated in 1912 by Queen Maria Cristina herself, it's since been visited by many other royals (often of the Hollywood variety). Set on the banks of the Urumea, with romantic river views from many of the rooms, the hotel is right in the thick of the city's celebrated architecture, food, and fun. Foodies will enjoy the in-house tributes to San Sebastián's culinary culture: gourmet cooking classes (try

the art of Iberian ham carving or paella making) and the stellar selection of pintxos, complete with wine pairings. *hotel-mariacristina.com/en*

EAT • Akelar̃e (translation: "witchcraft"), which boasts 3 of San Sebastián's 16 Michelin stars and offers a spectacular view of the sea to accompany your Nueva Cocina Vasca, or New Basque cuisine. Though the menu changes seasonally, past hits have included the grouper with

asparagus and the apple tart in edible paper. *akelarre.net/en*

PLAY • Climb a mountain. The city is surrounded by them, and not surprisingly, they serve up some of its best views. Start with Igueldo's Tower on the mountain of the same name for an amazing perspective on La Concha and the city. And if pintxo overload disincentivizes you from climbing, take the funicular railway (the Basque Country's oldest) to the top instead.

PORTUGAL
AZORES

Deep in the Atlantic, a Volcanic Island Idyll

Take a gorgeous, centuries-old Portuguese cityscape, airlift it about 900 miles offshore, drop it onto a bubbling, primordial volcanic cluster in the Atlantic, and you'll have a reasonable facsimile of the Azores. Still part of Portugal, seven centuries after the first colonists turned up with sheep and grapevines, these nine islands constitute Europe's westernmost outpost and wildest fusion of raw nature and continental culture. ✴ Conveniently, one of the best places to experience this blend is where you'll land: São Miguel, also known as the Green Island, and home to the Azorean capital of Ponta Delgada. Spend at least one afternoon wandering

the town center, where hallmarks include stark white walls accessorized by black volcanic rock, a colorful fishing harbor, and that most beautiful of Portuguese flourishes: swirling mosaic sidewalks.

Just beyond the city limits, you'll find the ravishing results of volcanic turmoil in almost any direction you go. Hit the

bubbly, steamy little town of Furnas to experience as much of the thermal circuit as possible. Highlights include the Caldeira Velha, where you can swim through a jungle-shrouded warm waterfall; Poça da Dona Beija, with a series of soaking pools alongside a sweet little stream; and the Terra Nostra Hotel, home to a massive thermal swimming pool and lush

---

Top left: Azores meets all your romantic needs: sun, soft-sand beaches, and plenty of water views. *Top middle:* While in Azores enjoy Portuguese dessert wine with tapas. *Top right:* Enjoy the Criação Velha wine region. *Opposite:* The lush Terra Nostra Botanical Gardens

botanical gardens. Inside the hotel you can feast on volcanically heated specialties—variations of the local *cozido* (or stew)—and take a class on how to make them.

The same forces that left Furnas so steamy created a complement of crater lakes you'll want to experience as well, whether on foot, on bike, or in the water. The most celebrated is Sete Cidades, with its lushly landscaped conjoined pools. When the light hits them just so, one looks green, while the other looks blue. According to one myth, when forbidden lovers—a green-eyed boy and blue-eyed girl—were forced to separate, each shed so many tears that the outpouring formed separate pools. Though lacking a beautiful backstory, Lagoa do Fogo (translation: "fire lake") is also worth a visit, particularly because of the mystical, Mordor-like landscape you'll trek through to get there.

You could happily spend your entire getaway on São Miguel, but you should also visit some other islands for variety's sake. If you have time for only one, head to Pico, whose namesake mountain is the tallest in Portugal. Coming to a dramatic, often mist-shrouded point, the mountain rewards hikers with astounding views of the neighboring islands. For a hike of a different kind, wend your way through Madalena's Criação Velha wine region. The vineyards' swirl of volcanic stone walls—built hundreds of years ago to protect the grapes from winds and sea surges—are still standing and fostering delicious wines. Have a taste at the Cellar Bar at the arresting new Lugar da Barca.

Another local specialty? Whale- and dolphin-watching. The area is host to more than 20 species, and the undisputed stars, giant sperm whales, hang out here all summer.

At day's end, you won't find a grander finale than the sunset from Lajes do Pico. Behind you: an old Portuguese fishing village. In front of you: the shimmering Atlantic. And right beside you: the person you're happiest to be sharing this beautiful blend with.

Featuring the best of both worlds, the Azores have both beach and green mountains on offer.

Opposite: São Nicolau church at Sete Cidades *Above:* Hike the rim of Lagoa do Fogo for remarkable vistas.

PLAN YOUR TRIP

STAY • Furnas Boutique Hotel, Thermal & Spa, named for the literal hot spot the hotel calls home. With a larger-than-life rendering of a local waterfall looming over the lobby, this beautifully designed new retreat in a 19th-century thermal bath center instantly sets the mood for exploring the surrounding landscape. Not surprisingly, there's a great thermal spa on the premises. *furnasboutiquehotel.com*

EAT • Fonte Cuisine Restaurant, housed in a secluded seaside estate, where you can sit on a leafy patio in the summer and enjoy such local specialties as the soft *queijo do pico* cheese and hearty fish soup. Afterward, stroll the bucolic grounds. You'll find paths that lead to the sea—and to an onsite whale-watching tower, where you may just spot a few dolphins and sperm whales. *aldeiadafonte.com*

PLAY • Take a dip in a natural swimming pool alongside the Atlantic. You'll find several of these "pocas," which are walled off by rocks and filled with ocean water, to swim in while you stay completely protected from the strong ocean currents. The most romantic option on Pico: the secluded Poça Branca, a natural swimming pool in Prainha. Or swim beneath a 300-foot waterfall in Poça do Bacalhau.

CHINA

YUNNAN PROVINCE

Mountains, Monasteries, and a Tantalizing Taste of Tibet

The only thing romance seekers need know before deciding to visit Yunnan: This province in the far southwest of China is home to Shangri-La. Yes, a cartographic entry actually reads "Shangri-La County" (or the Mandarin equivalent thereof). Granted the area used to go by other names, but after the world fell in love with the mythic Shangri-La—that Himalayan idyll of *Lost Horizon* fame—many a municipal government claimed to represent the real-life version, and petitioned Beijing for the accordant name change. And you'll see why the honor went to this stunning swath of Yunnan as soon as you arrive at your local digs (see **Stay**). ✴ You'll find a

Himalayan skyline, lush, misty slopes, Tibetan farmhouses, riverside yaks, and centuries-old Buddhist monasteries with fluttering multihued flags. In short: a ringer for James Hilton's utopia.

For a glorious overview, walk along the shores of the

crystalline Bita Lake, the highest in Yunnan and the so-called pearl on the plateau. (While you're here, keep your eyes and ears open for muntjacs, the small, stalky, and severely adorable creatures also known as barking deer—for good reason). Then visit the 17th-century Songzanlin

Top left: Red lanterns hang from restaurants in the old town of Lijiang. *Top middle:* Spend your evening around a bonfire hosted by the Banyan Tree Ringha. *Top right:* Songzanlin Temple (or Ganden Sumtseling Monastery) is a Tibetan Buddhist monastery in Shangri-La. *Opposite:* Dusk settles on the lantern-lit canals of Lijiang.

monastery, the largest Tibetan Buddhist center in the province and an architectural tribute to the Potala Palace. If you're feeling ambitious, drive north for a few hours past villages and dramatic limestone formations until you reach the Baima Mountain Pass, an alpine flora wonderland with virgin forests, golden monkeys, and, in summer, abundant azaleas.

At some point, you'll have to bid farewell to Shangri-La if you want to see more of Yunnan. And you should, considering what a visual and cultural treat the province can be. It's known for its mix of ethnic minorities, so traveling here means a series of new cuisines (see **Eat**), languages (Dongba, for example, is said to be the world's only actively maintained pictographic script), and outfits (the most arresting of which belong to the Yi women, who adorn themselves with satellite dish–like black hats).

The landscapes around Yunnan are equally amazing, as you'll find when you're walking through the Tiger Leaping Gorge, one of the deepest river canyons on Earth. Or staring at the glacial reflection of Jade Dragon Snow Mountain in the surface of Jade Spring Park's 18th-century Black Dragon Pool (*left*). Or riding a yak into the White Water River Terraces. Or surveying the First Bend of the Yangtze, where the river makes a famously breathtaking U-turn through lush willows, steep mountains, and old Tibetan homes.

Of course, the province isn't entirely pastoral. To get the full town-and-country experience, spend a day along the waterways and bridges of the UNESCO World Heritage–designated old town of Lijiang. And at night, watch the partiers who challenge each other—from open-air bars on either side of a canal—to singing duels. Not your run-of-the-mill utopia, to be sure—but fun nonetheless. Call it a Shangri-La for *Glee* fans.

At Black Dragon Pool Park, you can get front seats to Jade Dragon Snow Mountain views.

Opposite: A local woman carries hay in Shangri-La. *Above:* The Tibetan spa guest room at Banyan Tree Ringha

PLAN YOUR TRIP

STAY • Banyan Tree Ringha, a National Geographic Unique Lodge modeled after a traditional Tibetan farming village—an apt motif, given that this Himalayan hide-away is located in an ethnically Tibetan part of Yunnan. Sure, there are under-stated upgrades from your standard-issue farmhouse—pillow menus and spa-caliber soaking tubs, for example. But the village vibe remains intact, especially when colorfully clad local yak herders and their yaks promenade through the property en route to the neighboring river. *banyantree.com*

EAT • 1 Restaurant in Old Town Shuhe, serving up local, pan-Asian, and Naxi fare that's made with fresh-from-the-market ingredients. Set inside an old house with a terrace and flower-filled courtyard, the place is notoriously hard to find, but getting lost in Yunnan's old town is part of the fun.

4-14 Renli Road, Gucheng District, Lijiang

PLAY • Among the field trips on offer at the Banyan Tree, the Shangrila Culture Trek is a standout. After a lovely little hike, you'll be invited into a village home to try house-made yak cheese and yak butter tea (both kindly contributed by the yaks right out-side). You'll also visit an ancient pine forest and the neighborhood monastery: the 800-year-old Ringha Da Bao Si.

Autumn casts
Lake Bled, Slovenia,
in an array of colors.

FALL

ITALY

VENICE

The Most Romantic City in the World

It's Casanova's hometown, the birthplace of the celebrity courtesan—and, according to Shakespeare, the probable scene of Cupid's biggest shooting spree. Welcome to Venice, where romance has always had a flare for the unbridled—and shows no signs of slowing. ✳ So that gondola serenade you feared might be too clichéd? Totally happening. Ditto Bellinis at Harry's Bar and cappuccinos at Florian's, the latter founded in 1720 and still housed in the same elegant building on the Piazza San Marco. Chances are you'll simply have zero resistance to the city's romantic staples—which are, in fact, all they're cracked up to be. Especially when

you subtract the summer crowds and add some fresh fall air.

Of course, given Venice's 150 waterways, off-the-beaten-canal romance abounds, too. Consider the site that countless travelers photograph but few ever visit: the island and church of San Giorgio Maggiore, where you'll be dazzled by the views from the bell tower. Or attend a gloriously unconventional opera: At Musica a

Palazzo, seven performers stage each act in a different room. So you'll literally follow the action and occasionally wind up in it. In *La Traviata*, for example, you'll toast with Violetta as she's about to find love. Because in this city of over-the-top romance, why *wouldn't* you raise a glass with an iconic romantic heroine while she's singing one of opera's most beloved refrains?

Top left: Grab coffee for two at a café in the beautiful Piazza San Marco. *Top middle:* Arrive at St. Mark's Square at sunrise for spectacular sights and fewer crowds. *Top right:* Visit Burano for even more canal rides, with colorful homes along your way.

Canal views—and gondola visits—are abundant during dinner at Osteria da Fiore.

PLAN YOUR TRIP

STAY • The Gritti Palace, born in 1475 as the Venetian doge's residence, then reborn as the Vatican's ambassadors' home before becoming this beloved hotel in 1895. Among the names to fill the guest book are Bogart, Bacall, Churchill, Chaplin, Stravinsky, Springsteen, and Jagger. No two rooms are exactly alike, but some have Grand Canal views that you should request the moment you decide to book. *thegrittipalace.com*

EAT • Osteria da Fiore, which serves up canal views through flower-lined windows (book well in advance to score one of the two tables at the end of the dining room). Rivaling the scenery is the Michelin-starred menu, with such standouts as the bass in balsamic vinegar. *dafiore.net*

PLAY • Explore the canals and get some exercise in the bargain. Venice Kayak offers all manner of tours, from a loop around the Technicolor island of Burano to an extra-romantic nighttime paddle on the Grand Canal. If one of you is a beginner—or you simply can't get enough of each other—book a tandem kayak. *venicekayak.com*

CALIFORNIA

BIG SUR

Where Quiet Coves Double as Treasure Troves

Aqua coves dot the shores of Big Sur, as seen from Julia Pfeiffer Burns State Park.

Though the magic of Big Sur defies description, many spellbound writers have tried anyway—perhaps most successfully, onetime novelist-in-residence Henry Miller: "Big Sur is the California that men dreamed of years ago; this is the Pacific that Balboa looked at from the Peak of Darien . . . the face of the earth as the Creator intended it to look." * Indeed, there's something primal about Big Sur's beauty. The all-but-untouched Santa Lucia Mountains plunge into the Pacific, forming coves of sparkling aquamarine. The redwoods soar into the stratosphere, their canopy so dense in places that the time of day becomes a matter of pure

conjecture. And all the while, whales patrol the coast, their mighty sprays dancing in the golden sunlight.

Although this place is transcendent year-round, it's arguably at its best in fall. The weather's still warm, but the summer fog has cleared, leaving (mostly) sunny skies by day and starry ones by night. Then there's the wildlife. Joining the blue whales, humpbacks, and orcas that have already been here a few months are the migratory hummingbirds—plus the thousands of monarch butterflies that gather for an October summit at Andrew Molera State Park each year.

Driving along the coast and making frequent stops at the scenic overlooks is the traditional way to enjoy all of the

Go early to Sierra Mar restaurant at the Post Ranch Inn to grab an outdoor table and enjoy the sunset.

above. And rightly so, as you'll discover, among other places, 13 miles south of Carmel, where you'll come to the Bixby Bridge, one of the highest single-span concrete arch bridges ever built.

Still, hiking has its own considerable payoffs as well. As inaccessible as Big Sur's coves look from the cliffs above, some beaches can be reached on foot. Walk the Jade Cove Trail, for example, and you'll get wide-open coastal views before descending to the beach to hunt for jade (yes, there's actual jade on these shores). Or take the Sand Dollar Beach Trail down to the area's most sweeping sandy stretch, and search for even more of the gorgeous green treasure.

Also on offer are treks through the trees. The Pfeiffer Falls & Valley View hike in Pfeiffer Big Sur State Park, for one, gets you up close and personal with the giant redwoods and a bonus waterfall. If you want to keep going, continue to the overlook of the Big Sur River gorge.

The best local remedy for hike-weary quads? Hot springs. The mineral-rich pools at the Esalen Institute are known as much for their location on an oceanside cliff as for their healing properties. And should Esalen's clothing-optional policy give you pause, keep in mind that the baths are open to the public only after dark, from one o'clock to three o'clock in the morning.

Large redwood forests make for excellent hiking.

So if, in the spirit of Henry Miller, you decide to go with the early Genesis-era dress code—not so much as a fig leaf—no one will be the wiser.

PLAN YOUR TRIP

STAY • Post Ranch Inn, where you'll get the most coveted views in the neighborhood from the swanky cottages that cling to soaring, oceanside cliffs. (Request one of these, rather than a tree house, if you want to look out on the water.) Though your own private hot tub will have unreal views, you'll also want to soak in the large, communal infinity hot tub that's perched atop the Pacific and surrounded by riotously landscaped gardens. The property also has

several hiking trails and a couples spa suite that overlooks a redwood grove. *postranchinn.com*

EAT • Nepenthe, a beloved local eatery, which sits right off the coastal highway on cliffs that overlook the ocean. Here, you'll find legendary burgers and even more legendary views, the latter starring the Santa Lucias and maybe a passing whale or two. *nepenthebigsur.com*

PLAY • Head 25 miles north to experience the California coast's celebrated 17-Mile Drive. Opened in the 1880s, this gated road originally served as a scenic carriage ride for the well-heeled guests of Monterey's Hotel Del Monte. Today, for a toll of about $10, anyone can enter to see the highlights, which include the fabled old Lone Cypress, Pebble Beach, the Del Monte Forest, Pacific Grove, and Bird Rock.

INDIA
KERALA

Mystical Culture, Magical Nature

Hindu tradition holds that when the sixth incarnation of the almighty Mahavishnu threw his ax into the advancing seas, Kerala sprang up. But even if you didn't know this backstory, the area's alias, God's own country, would make perfect sense. Flanked by the Arabian Sea and the Western Ghats range, laced with almost 50 rivers, and carpeted in forests and plantations, this southwestern Indian state has the indisputable look and feel of a divine playground. ∗ So fertile is this soil, in fact, that Kerala was a hub of the ancient spice route that spanned Asia, Africa, and Europe. And to this day, you'll find some of India's freshest, most flavorful food here.

Black pepper, cinnamon, cloves, and chili star in many of the regional dishes. But ironically, the one you may become most addicted to, the pudding-like *payasam* (fittingly derived from the Hindi word for "ambrosia"), isn't spicy at all. Nearly every establishment serves its own version of the state's signature

dessert, and you'll find yourselves picking a new favorite daily.

Fabulous food isn't the only offshoot of Kerala's fertility: The state is also said to be the birthplace of Ayurveda. Technically considered a form of medicine, the practice uses every local ingredient from cardamom to coconuts, and involves treatments

---

Top left: A nutmeg plant opened on Philipkutty's Farm in the backwaters of Kerala.
Top middle: A mother and daughter don saris. *Top right:* Find fresh fruits, like these hanging bananas, in Kerala's open-air markets.
Opposite: Houseboats along the Kerala backwaters are the height of comfortable cruising.

so tantalizing (the continuous drizzle of warm oil onto your "third eye" during a massage, for example) that you'll sign up whether or not you're in need of retuning.

Duly refreshed, you'll be ready for a backwater tour. Your home for the duration will be a refitted traditional rice boat, once key to the local agricultural economy. You'll explore a maze of emerald waterways, each fringed with palms and the occasional idyllic village. And for maximum romance, you can spend the night in this surreal setting (see **Play**).

Back on terra firma, don't miss Kerala's tea plantations. Set in the fabled hill stations of the Western Ghats, these misty, swirling seas of green, occasionally accented by waterfalls, are as much a feast for the eyes as for the palate. So make sure to taste local offerings: Though it's a bit of a trek at 8,000 feet above sea level, Kolukkumalai Tea Estate outside Munnar is not only the world's highest organic tea plantation but arguably the most beautiful.

The urban centers are every bit as dazzling—not least, Kochi (also known as Cochin). A magical melting pot thanks to its spice route origins, the city has gorgeous vestiges of the historic Jewish community (the crystal-bedecked Paradesi synagogue, for one, is the oldest still in use in India). You can also find traces of the Portuguese, Dutch, and British communities, whose colonial stints left behind beautiful architecture, and of the Chinese community, whose traditional stilted fishing nets are, oddly, among the most romantic sights you'll see, especially at sunset.

While you're in town, catch a show at the Kathakali Centre. You can (and should) go early to watch the actors transform into elaborately made up and costumed characters who emote and gesticulate wildly through ancient dance-dramas. As befits a performance in God's own country, the action will be lifted from a sacred text—and your post-show photo session with the green-faced star will be the perfect taste of divine madness.

The Chinese fishing nets that line the piers of Kochi (Cochin) make the sunsets even more magical.

Opposite: Tea plantations cover the landscape of Munnar. *Above:* The deluxe allure suite at Vivanta by Taj-Kumarakom

PLAN YOUR TRIP

STAY • Vivanta by Taj-Kumarakom, housed in a 150-year-old missionary's cottage on the lush banks of Vembanad Lake. One of the best things to do here is watch as a thousand lamps are lit around the property nightly until the whole place seems to be flickering. Arguably as magical is a treatment at the Ayurvedic spa—and a stay in one of the Premium Temptation Villas, each with a private veranda plunge pool, Jacuzzi, open-air garden shower, and Kerala coir swing. *vivanta.tajhotels.com*

EAT • Menorah, in an atmospheric Kochi mansion, where you will have been preceded by prime ministers, viceroys, ambassadors, Nobel laureates, and Hollywood royalty. In a nod to the once prominent Jewish family that used to live here, you'll find Semitic South Indian specialties from sumptuously spiced chicken dishes to a special version of payasam. *koderhouse.com*

PLAY • Book a Taj houseboat for a cruise along Kerala's backwaters. Adapted from the region's historic rice boats, today's versions come with bathrooms, an open lounge, a deck, air-conditioned sleeping quarters, a kitchen, and your own chef. There's no more decadent way to take in the views.

SOUTHERN ISRAEL AND JORDAN

Experience a Romance of Biblical Proportions

A ridgetop view of the high-saline
waters of the Dead Sea in Israel

For romance of literally biblical proportions, head to southern Israel and Jordan. With desertscapes so dramatic that they've doubled for Mars on the big screen, the area is totally transcendent whatever your spiritual beliefs. A neighborhood border crossing, known as Yitzhak Rabin Terminal on the Israeli side and Wadi Araba on the Jordanian side, will keep your travels seamless. * Wherever you roam between the two, you'll be joining an illustrious, millennia-old visitor's list. King David, for example, is on record as having beaten you to Israel's Ein Gedi Nature Reserve by about 3,000 years. But whereas he had to hide out in the local caves, you'll

have the run of this amazing oasis, where the leafy river, falls, and natural pools cut a shockingly lush figure through the otherwise desolate landscape.

In its earliest appearances in Genesis, the nearby Dead Sea comes with no references to best floating practices. But subsequent generations have figured out that to enjoy this hypersaline solution 1,400 feet below sea level, you shouldn't shave for at least two days before you go in. This way, you can sit or lie on the surface of the water for hours, side by side or back to back, sans stinging. To up the therapeutic factor, the resorts that line the sea's periphery stock muds to slather yourselves in. This exercise in primordial pampering is magnified by the look of the sea,

The Beresheet Hotel offers an oasis—including large rooms, endless views, and a pool—in the desert atmosphere.

a crystalline whitish blue that doesn't seem quite of this world—especially at sunrise and sunset, both must-sees.

Another sunrise view not to be missed: the one from the top of Masada, King Herod's fortress. Get to the base at least an hour before dawn to hike the winding 1,300-foot Snake Path to the top. Once you've summited, the big show will include a pinkening Dead Sea and endless desert panorama. The ruins, which you can tour once the sun is up, are otherworldly as well, especially the ethereally illuminated great cistern.

To experience another millennia-old irrigation system, taste your way through the Negev wine route (good stops include Yatir, Kadesh Barnea, and Sde Boker Winery). Eventually you'll make your way to the border area of Eilat and Aqaba, where the Red Sea beckons snorkelers, divers, and swimmers. After you've had your share, one of the most extraordinary spectacles of your lives awaits: Petra.

This millennia-old Nabataean masterpiece, a vast series of temples, tombs, and monasteries carved into pinkish red sandstone cliffs and surrounded by mountains, was once a caravan city. Long since abandoned, its intricate passages and gorges could easily occupy you for an entire day. But for the hyper-romantic version, go back at night—an option on Mondays, Wednesdays, and Thursdays, when the Treasury (the most legendary of Petra's buildings) will be illuminated with the light

Candlelight shines on Petra's Treasury building.

of 1,500 candles (*above*). It's a view you won't soon forget. And take it from us: This experience will highlight the role this trip has played in the—um—genesis of your relationship.

PLAN YOUR TRIP

STAY • The Beresheet Hotel, which overlooks the Makhtesh Ramon, a massive, crater-like depression in the desert floor. Staying here, you have the feeling that you're alone at the edge of the world, except for the odd ibex or gazelle. Book a crater-view room with a balcony or private pool to amplify that effect—although the view from the hotel pool is pretty hard to beat. *isrotel.com/beresheet*

EAT • The Cave Bar, which—at around 2,000 years old—is the self-declared oldest bar in the world. Part of the Petra ruins, this romantic retreat full of evocatively lit nooks has been refurbished since its early days as a Nabataean rock tomb and now serves up drinks and local specialties, along with some post-Petra-trekking comfort food (think falafel and potato wedges). *guesthouse-petra.com*

PLAY • Take a jeep, horse, or camel through Jordan's otherworldly Wadi Rum, the backdrop for every movie from *Lawrence of Arabia* to *The Martian*. Also known as the Valley of the Moon, this southern Jordan desert will awe and inspire with its sheer sandstone and granite mountains. After your tour, head to a Bedouin encampment, where you can have tea and stare up at the sea of flickering stars.

FRANCE
BURGUNDY

Beauty in a Bottle

"O blessed Burgundy . . . well worthy of being called the mother of men, she who possesses such milk in her veins." So wrote the famed 15th-century priest and theologian Erasmus of Rotterdam, who wasn't necessarily given to hyperbole. This central swath of France is indeed the most heavenly place to experience through wine—and nowhere more so than on the Route des Grands Crus. ✱ Dubbed the Champs-Élysées of Burgundy, these 40 or so mythic miles wend through a succession of towns and villages where the signposts read like a who's who of celebrated wine producers: Chambolle-Musigny, Vosne-Romanée, Nuits-Saint-Georges.

Not surprisingly, the place is hopping during the fall harvest, and though the local vineyards will have their hands full with, well, grape picking, you'll still find plenty of tasting opportunities. As you make your way along the route, look for degustation (tasting) callouts—or for their visual shorthand, a barrel topped with wine bottles. A few renowned tasting stops not to miss: the Château de Corton-André and cellars that once belonged to the Duke of Burgundy's Parliament; Maison Joseph Drouhin, where Thomas Jefferson precedes you in the guest book; and Château de Santenay, the former

---

Top left: It's easy to spot wine-tasting menus, which are in abundance throughout Burgundy. *Top middle:* Enjoy the sights cycling along the canals outside the village of Saint-Victor-sur-Ouche. *Top right:* At harvesttime you can watch grape picking in action.
Opposite: Near the Place de la Libération in Dijon, the food is just as good as the wine.

home of Philip the Bold, son of King John the Good of France.

However delightful the roadside tastings, you'll want to hit at least one harvest festival to experience the full breadth of local merriment—music, food, wine, the works. Though there are plenty of tempting options throughout the season, November's Les Trois Glorieuses (or Three Glories) is one for the books. Timed to the medieval city of Beaune's epic wine auction, reputedly the oldest such auction in the world, the festival includes winemakers' meals, cellar tours, and—once enough wine has flowed—group singing.

Even if you don't make the festival, visit the spot where the auction takes place: the Hospices de Beaune, a 15th-century almshouse turned museum. The countless treasures housed under its roof are rivaled only by what's *on* the roof. The polychromatic tile patterns here are some of the most beautiful you'll see in a region that's filled with—and known for—them. In fact, you'll find similarly fetching examples of the local tile work atop many wine castles (the Château de Corton André, for example). Back inside, be sure to take in the expansive 15th-century ceiling of the Room of the Poor. Each of the exposed beams features sculpted caricatures of Beaune's most important residents.

For all the region's wine heritage, recent history has given rise to a foodie scene that rivals the vines, with the stunning city of Dijon at the epicenter. Work up an appetite by touring the extra-opulent Palace of the Dukes of Burgundy, the Gothic Dijon cathedral, and the beautiful ex-monastery that is the Chartreuse de Champmol. Then get down to the very serious business of feasting (see **Eat**).

Keeping the consumption in check, Burgundy is a biking bastion too—especially on crisp, cool fall days. There are hundreds of miles of trails to choose from, many winding through the vineyards of Côte de Nuits and Côte de Beaune—just in case your veins aren't sufficiently filled with, as Erasmus would say, mother's milk.

Autumn hues decorate the vineyards overlooking Pernand-Vergelesses.

Opposite: A statue of lovers inside the Abbaye de la Bussière hotel *Above:* The Palace of the Dukes and the Place de la Libération in Dijon

PLAN YOUR TRIP

STAY • Abbaye de la Bussière, a respect-fully reimagined 12th-century monastery on bucolic grounds that feels more like a pal-ace (down to the miniature ponies) than a priory. You'll also find weeping willows, topiaries, and an ornamental lake. Not to be outdone, the guest rooms include vaulted ceilings, crystal chandeliers, toile galore, and en suite whirlpool baths. *abbayedelabussiere.fr*

EAT • La Maison des Cariatides, named for the female figures who adorn the facade of this 17th-century Dijonnais wine merchant's house turned Michelin-starred restaurant in the heart of the old city. Set against a back-drop of softly lit stone walls and a small open kitchen, it has a tasting menu that changes daily but always fuses fresh local ingredients with interesting imports (think Dijon meets dashi). *lamaisondescariatides.fr*

PLAY • Spend three days to a week cruising the bucolic Burgundy canal on a barge. You may want to charter your own so you can stop, stroll, bike, and sip wherever you choose. Without even leaving the boat, you'll see the Cister-cian Abbey of Fontenay, plus a whole succession of châteaus: Bussy, Tanlay, and Ancy le Franc among them. *hotelsafloat.com*

CZECH REPUBLIC

PRAGUE

A Golden City of Music, Culture, and Love

Bridges cross Prague's Vltava
River, seen here at night.

As if the Golden City of 100 Spires weren't sufficiently romantic on its own, the fabled autumn light—a trick of the sun's seasonally low angle—gilds the whole scene a second time over and leaves you putty in Prague's hands. ∗ And wait until you factor in the other pleasures of the season. As the cultural calendar reignites, for example, the per capita concert rates go from merely *high* to holy-Amadeus-where-do-we-begin? (Mozart is a particular local favorite, given his 18th-century love affair with the city.) ∗ Your best musical starting point may well be the storied Estates Theatre, where Wolfgang himself conducted the premiere of *Don Giovanni*

in October 1787. This operatic take on Don Juan remains a fixture on the theater's annual list of offerings, as does Mozart's beloved romantic comedy *Le Nozze di Figaro,* among other classics. For purer romance, however, see if you can find a performance of his *Prague* Symphony (official name: Symphony No. 38) in town. Chances are good, as you'll discover from the ever changing concert flyers that flood the local kiosks and bulletin boards daily.

That flood graduates to a deluge once the fall music festivals roll into town, starting with Dvořák's. A 19th-century hometown boy made good, he's still revered as a hero of the Romantic era and celebrated throughout September with a lineup of not only his own work but that of his contemporaries and students. Then there's Strings of Autumn, a genre-bending festival that has showcased everyone from jazz vocalist Bobby McFerrin to actress Ute Lemper and runs from September to November.

You'll have no problems cozying up to one another in a room at the Four Seasons Prague.

And from early October through early November, you can catch the International Jazz Festival Praha, one of the oldest in the country, with Louis Armstrong and the Duke Ellington Orchestra among the earliest headliners.

The city's visual arts shine in autumn as well, in one case, literally. For part of October, you can see several of the city's landmarks in a whole new light when the Signal Festival illuminates them with splashy colors every evening; you need only walk around the Old Town by the river to catch the show. October also brings the Four Days Festival, a provocative blend of video art, contemporary dance, and other visual and theatrical pieces.

Of course, some of the city's best displays require no staging. October is prime time for local leaf peeping, and Petrin Hill, the highest in the city at 1,072 feet, is the perfect vantage point (and, not altogether incidentally, a local make-out point). Located above the left bank of the Vltava River and almost entirely filled with parks, the peak is a Prague favorite. Hike or take the funicular up, and you'll be blinded by the copper, crimson, and yellow below.

Or just go for the romantic jugular and take a walk across the Vltava on the Charles Bridge. This 15th-century span isn't merely atmospheric; it's lined with statues of saints, one of whom is said to be able to make your heart's desires come true.

Gourmet treats await at U Zlaté Studně.

His name is St. John of Nepomuk and you can't miss him. The spot where he's been polished by the hands of a million supplicants becomes a beacon in the golden autumn light.

PLAN YOUR TRIP

STAY • The Four Seasons, a trio of converted historical buildings—one baroque, one neoclassical, and one neo-Renaissance—in the middle of the Old Town. But despite the exquisite architecture and plush accommodations, this place is all about the views. Ask for a Premier River Room or one of the river-facing suites to get views of the Vltava and Malá Strana district, as well as the Charles Bridge or Prague Castle. Or simply book the Presidential or Premier Suite to get all of the above. *fourseasons.com*

EAT • U Zlaté Studně, a 1528 aerie on a hillside near Prague Castle. From here, the views of the city's rooftops are so jaw-dropping that eating may be a problem—and more's the pity: The restaurant has snagged awards for such signatures as Angus steak with foie gras rougié, truffled potato puree, and Baron Philippe de Rothschild Sauternes sauce. *goldenwell.cz/dining-en.html*

PLAY • Once the sun is down, experience an autumn glow of a different kind: a river cruise through the floodlit fantasia that is Prague by night. On your evening ride, take in the wonder of the glowing Prague Castle as you float beneath the Charles Bridge, and toast each other as you sail by the baroque Lesser Town and Old Town churches.

ITALY

TUSCANY

Olive Groves and Vineyards, Medieval Villages and World-Class Art

The hills of Tuscany
glow in the sunset.

If you ever decide to revisit the romantic canon, you'll find that most works feature one hero and one heroine. But in E. M. Forster's A Room With a View, *there's an equally important third character: Florence. Lucy Honeychurch, perhaps Forster's most celebrated romantic heroine, even likens the city to another woman: "Was there more to her beauty than met the eye? The power, perhaps, to evoke passions . . . and to bring them to speedy fulfillment?"* ✽ *The answer, of course, is yes. And that power shoots straight through the fabled City of Lilies and into the Tuscan countryside—especially in fall, when the harvest is in full swing. Make sure*

Outdoor cafés are abundant on the streets of Pietrasanta.

to block out a few luxurious days in each area to experience the full range of local delights.

In Florence, one of the best places to retreat on a crisp autumn day is the sprawling Boboli Gardens behind the Pitti Palace, old stomping grounds of the Medicis. Dating back to the 16th century, the gardens are filled with Roman statues, mannerist sculptures, fanciful fountains, and grottoes that beg for stolen kisses. An especially private section that's likely—as Lucy would say—to bring passion to speedy fulfillment: the sloped series of leafy tunnels between Porta Romana and the hilltop.

While you're in Oltrarno—the neighborhood on the "other" (less trafficked) side of the Arno River—make sure to visit a postcard photographers' favorite vantage point: the sumptuous, high-up Piazzale Michelangelo, marked by a bronze replica of the David. Here, you'll find impressive views of Santa Croce,

PLAN YOUR TRIP

STAY Castello di Casole—a Timbers Resort. This millennium-old, 4,200-acre hilltop estate is filled with olive groves, grape vines, and cypress colonnades—and lots of romantic lore. Long a refuge for Sienese political exiles and aristocrats, the castle was eventually bought by Italian film legend Luchino Visconti, who entertained Elizabeth Taylor, among others, here. For romance of a less glam, more earthy sort, plan your visit during the grape and olive harvest in September; you'll be invited to get your hands dirty and help pick both crops. But keep in mind that the winter season arrives early here. The hotel, like much of rural Tuscany, shuts down in November. *castellodicasole.com*

Ancient archways border the
Piazza dell'Anfiteatro.

Castello di Casole offers some of the greatest views of Tuscany's rolling hills.

the sculptor's final resting place, as well as the celebrated Uffizi gallery, the elaborately adorned Duomo, the ancient arcaded Ponte Vecchio bridge, and the purple mountains that recede into the distance.

Another attraction you shouldn't miss while you're up here: the stunning San Miniato al Monte, dating to the 11th century and widely considered one of Italy's finest Romanesque churches. Make sure to stop by the graveyard, where you'll find the tombstone of none other than Carlo Lorenzini, aka Carlo Collodi, who created Pinocchio.

Back on the other side of the Arno—once you've completed the obligatory circuit of the sublime (the Academia, Uffizi, Santa Croce, and Ponte Vecchio)—climb to the top of the Duomo (the soaring red dome was designed by Fillipo Brunelleschi) for aptly divine city views. Then stroll along the river until you happen upon the perfect place to watch the sun set—ideally, on a wall of one of the city's ancient bridges. (Once again, *A Room With a View* comes to mind: "Evening approached . . . the colours on the trees and hills were purified, and the Arno lost its muddy solidity and began to twinkle.")

This beauty has been known to elicit tears, as has leaving it. But decamping for the country comes with its own rewards—among them, Tuscany's surplus of blissful hot springs. Some of the most celebrated are the Terme di Saturnia, named for the Roman harvest god whose handiwork you'll see in the neighborhood's hilltop vineyards. Make your way to the cascading pools by the old mill (or the Cascate del Mulino)—as much for the setting as the warm waters. Equally beautiful and fun to soak

PLAN YOUR TRIP

EAT Il Palagio, a decadent retreat in Florence. Under the vaulted ceilings and period chandeliers of the Palazzo della Gherardesca you'll enjoy Michelin-starred specialties such as sea bass fillet with an olive crust on creamed artichokes, the best local wines, and views of the gorgeous gardens. *ilpalagioristorante.it*

The Ponte Vecchio bridge in Florence, as seen from Piazzale Michelangelo, is filled with shop stalls.

in are the whitewashed Fosso Bianco pools in Bagni San Filippo.

In fact, Tuscany serves up so many different kinds of romance that you'll want to experience the complete tasting menu. Consider, for example, hearing a Puccini opera live in the composer's medieval hometown of Lucca. His music is performed here nightly through October (and a few nights a week thereafter) thanks to the annual festival that bears his name. Most of the events take place in San Giovanni Basilica, where the composer was baptized.

You'll also want to explore the vineyards that have helped make Tuscany famous—so consider harvest hopping on horseback. Equestrian wine tourism is popular in the area, and

typically includes not just vineyards and tasting rooms but olive groves, hilltop villages, medieval castles, and country churches. And if you go early enough in autumn, you'll probably ride by

PLAN YOUR TRIP

PLAY Sign up for a do-it-yourself potable souvenir of your trip. Through the Winemaker for a Day program in Radda, you'll taste several varietals directly from their aging barrels. Then, in an ancient room filled with high-tech equipment, you'll blend different percentages until you find a mix you both love. Your creation will be bottled, custom-labeled, aged for about a month, and shipped to you. *discoveryouritaly.com*

at least a few hustling grape pickers. You may even be able to lend a hand (see **Stay**).

Though wine and romance pair endlessly in Tuscany, you can't get a higher dose of either than at the Enoteca Italiana. In medieval Siena, a city that rivals Florence in brilliance and beauty, you'll find that the cellar and dungeon of this former Medici fortress have been transformed into a wine wonderland, complete with bar, shop, restaurant, and the occasional class. More than 1,500 bottles represent nearly every varietal in Italy—so show up thirsty.

Conveniently, the medieval city walls form an elegant containment system, allowing you to stray only so far during your post-tasting stroll. Make sure to visit the black-and-white striped Duomo, where the bewitching cupola is topped only (and literally) by Bernini's celebrated golden lantern. And hit at least a couple of the local palazzi (the 13th-century Tolomei and 14th-century Comunale are good starting points). But the one place you can't miss is the central, UNESCO World Heritage–designated Piazza del Campo, a particular favorite of posing brides and grooms. So if you're not already married or engaged, the wine, the wedding photographers, and the romantic power of Tuscany may just change your status on the spot.

Ride a moped through the streets of Florence to find hidden artwork throughout the city walls.

BHUTAN

A Himalayan Kingdom of Natural Beauty

Despite making international headlines for its Gross National Happiness indicators, Bhutan is at least as remarkable for its Gross National Beauty. For a country about half the size of Indiana, this Buddhist kingdom tucked deep into the heart of the Himalaya boasts a staggering array of breathtaking scenery. Along with the epic snowy peaks you might expect, there are also lush tropical and subtropical landscapes, ravishing misty river valleys and dense pine forests. To say nothing of the embarrassment of man-made riches that come in the form of fortresses and monasteries. ✳ The most famous of the latter, the Tiger's Nest Monastery,

should be one of the first items on your agenda. The very embodiment of Bhutan's impossible allure, the holiest site in the land is built on a series of cliff-top ledges 10,000 feet above sea level. And though you'll have to ascend 1,000 or so stairs to get here (or secure a mule to do the honors), the views along the way—forested slopes, prayer flag–

draped pines, and the monastery itself—are well worth the effort.

If you go to only one other religious establishment while you're here, make it Chimi Lhakhang, the temple of the Drukpa Kunley. Unless, of course, you don't want to have children. The story goes that between the 15th and 16th centuries, the

---

Top left: The ornate interior of Bukhari Restaurant at Uma Paro Resort *Top middle:* Gold Buddhist praying wheels in Bhutan *Top right:* Dancers wear traditional masks and costumes during the Punakha Dzong festival. *Opposite:* Young monks stand by colorful procession flags.

Bhutanese patron saint (the so-called Divine Madman) used his, um, "thunderbolt" to solve the country's most pressing issues, from demons to infertility. So when you visit his temple as a couple, a monk will give you a fertility-enhancing tap on the head with a wooden likeness of said thunderbolt—an experience you won't forget, any more than you will the ardent devotion and lamplit beauty of this place. The visit will also go a long way toward explaining the festooned phalluses you'll notice on walls and roofs all over the country. (No, you're not seeing things.)

Equally impressive are Bhutan's fortress-like *dzongs*: military, administrative, and religious hybrid institutions that dot the landscape with their high, inward-sloping white walls, red accents, outsize entryways, and interior courtyards, they add gravity and beauty to the Himalayan scenery. Arguably the most beautiful is the 17th-century Punakha Dzong, where every Bhutanese king has been crowned. Of course, its position at the confluence of the Pho Chhu (father) and Mo Chhu (mother) rivers doesn't hurt the aesthetic—but then, neither do the fortress's three courtyards, gold-domed central tower, and intricately carved chapel.

After you've experienced the joys of traditional Bhutanese architecture, make sure to explore the surrounding landscape—one of the region's main attractions. To enjoy the scenery at its purest, try a trek. You'll find options of every length: short (the two-day hike from Thimpu to Punakha through villages, forests, and rice fields), medium (the six-day Dagala Thousand Lakes Trek, with Himalayan views that include Everest), and long (the 14-day Laya-Gasa Trek, a blend of alpine meadows, mountain passes, and subtropical jungle). To soothe your muscles afterward, take a local hot stone bath for two. You'll be soaking in fresh river water that's been mixed with artemisia leaves and heated with fire-roasted stones—the sum total of which will send your Gross *Personal* Happiness off the charts.

Private dining can be arranged in the courtyard of Uma by COMO, Paro, catered by Bukhari Restaurant.

Opposite: A monk walks through Punakha Temple. *Above:* Buddhist prayer flags flutter outside Tiger's Nest Monastery.

PLAN YOUR TRIP

STAY • Zhiwa Ling, a National Geographic Unique Lodge in the hills outside Paro, where hand-decorated, intricately carved cottages are cloistered among resident weeping willows and fruit trees. Whether you join the monks at the Meditation House, while away the afternoons in the Tea House, get pampered at the spa, or have cocktails at the Mad Monk Bar, the serenity is unprecedented—as are the views, which include the Tiger's Nest Monastery. *zhiwaling.com*

EAT • Bukhari, a circular wood-and-glass restaurant in the town of Paro, is your best shot at rubbing shoulders with the Bhutanese aristocracy. This is the royal family's local restaurant of choice—and not just because of the 360-degree forest views. The menu relies heavily on ingredients from the kitchen's own organic garden, which is run in cooperation with area farmers, so the flavors are spectacularly fresh. If you go at lunch, try the yak burger.

comohotels.com/umaparo/dining/bukhari

PLAY • Hit a festival, many of which happen in the fall. The Bhutanese calendar is lunar, so you'll have to check for exact dates when you're planning your trip, but October and November should offer up a number of options. Try to attend the Pema Gatshel Tshechu, whose pageantry alone is worth the trip. Windhorse Tours can help you organize accordingly. *windhorsetours.com*

WESTERN SLOVENIA

Caves, Castles, and an Enchanted Lake

The Church of Assumption on
the small island in Lake Bled

Ljubljana is as love-centric as a town can be: The main square honors the 19th-century bard France Prešeren, whose love poems made him a national hero. In fact, a terra-cotta likeness of his muse still peers out on the square from the window of the palace she grew up in. And even if you've never heard of Prešeren or his love, you'll thank the revered poet for setting the stage here. ∗ Despite being a cosmopolitan capital this city has an ethereal feel—especially when you walk along the café-lined riverbanks at night, when the stone walls of the 15th-century Ljubljana Castle are floodlit in a slow progression of gold, blue, and indigo. But don't admire

this citadel just from afar: Hike or take the funicular up during the day and you'll be rewarded with dramatic city views. They're even better when you pair them with alfresco wine (or coffee and cake) from the café at the castle. To go a bit deeper into the site's history, take one of the daily "classic" tours of the grounds. Or opt for the more sporadic "Time Machine" tour,

a history of six key periods of Ljubljana as told by characters in period costume.

But the dreamiest of Slovenian destinations, together with Ljubljana, form a little circuit in the west. Stop number one: the ravishingly beautiful town of Bled, where the setting more than makes up for the unfortunate nomenclature. At the heart of the

Walkways border Lake Bled, making it easy to take hand-in-hand strolls and enjoy the stunning scenery.

town is a shimmering lake bordered by a cliff-top medieval castle and punctuated by an enisled church—all of this set against a backdrop of some of the highest peaks in the Julian Alps.

During the 1950s through the 1970s, when Slovenia was part of Josip Broz Tito's Yugoslavia, Bled was among one of the autocrat's favorite escapes. And the area has holdovers from not only his days here (see **Stay**) but from centuries past. The Pletna boats that dot the lake, for example, date back to the 16th century. (Their awnings and oarsmen add an especially nostalgic touch to your must-do romantic cruise.) And be sure to walk all the way around the church once you dock at the little island, where you don't want to miss a single view. Then there's Bled Castle, a medieval fortress turned museum, built on a precipice over the lake. With two courtyards, winding staircases, a drawbridge, and a moat, the repurposed royal residence (see **Eat**) has a fairy-tale vibe. Visit at sunset for particularly stunning views.

The next stops on your Slovenian circuit are two vastly different though equally impressive caves. At Postojna, chamber after chamber of hallucinatory, often glittering formations await (the cave is also home to oddly adorable blind salamanders). Predjama, by contrast, is a castle built into a cliff above a cave system—and the world's largest cave castle, according to Guinness World Records.

But even if you don't hit all three stops, you could wander

Rock formations inside the ethereal Postojna Caves

almost anywhere in this region and be awed: The same surreal beauty that inspired France Prešeren two centuries ago remains in full view today.

PLAN YOUR TRIP

STAY • Vila Bled, Tito's former vacation home. Given that "the Marshal" lived legendarily large, you'll find no shortage of epic views on these lakeside grounds. The best is from the Presidential Suite, once Tito's own quarters. But many a lake-facing room will let you look out across the sparkling water to the Julian Alps. *brdo.si/en/vila-bled/vila-bled*

EAT • Bled Castle Restaurant, which —despite being housed in a stronghold that dates back to the 11th century—serves up 21st-century takes on Slovenian staples (such as sausage and asparagus), along with breathtaking lake and island views. *jezersek.si/en/bled-castle-restaurant*

PLAY • Go even farther west. On the Roundabout Karst and Coast Mystery Tour, you'll journey to the Adriatic Sea via the Skocjan Caves, a UNESCO World Heritage site, one of the largest known underground canyons in the world, and home to a stunning subterranean river. After stopping for air-dried prosciutto and Teran wine—both specialties of the local Karst region—you'll head past the coastal towns of Koper, Izola, and Portoroz until you reach Piran. In this beloved medieval town, you can walk through the narrow, winding streets before settling in for a seafood feast by the Adriatic. *travel-slovenia.com*

SOUTH AMERICA
PERU
Dramatic Mountain Majesty

Once upon a time, there was a beautiful Inca princess who—despite having been promised to the Sun God—fell for a brave warrior. When her father discovered the affair and banished the young man, she ran away, shedding orchid-filled tears that blanketed the Andes with love. Indeed, the romance that permeates this part of the world is explained by countless local backstories—and you'll be willing to buy into almost any of them the moment you fall under the spell of Peru's misty mountains and haunting ruins. ✳ The gateway to the most fabled stretch of the Peruvian Andes lies in the country's southeastern region, about 11,000 feet above sea level.

Far more than a hub town, Cusco was once the epicenter of the Inca Empire and is now an arresting mash-up of indigenous stonework and Spanish colonial architecture. To experience one of the most decadent takes on this blend, head to Palacio Nazarenas, a centuries-old convent turned hotel, for a couples

massage at the resident spa. The glass cutouts in the floor of your treatment room will reveal ancient flowing Inca canals while you're facedown on the tables.

Happily refreshed, head next door to the Monasterio, another ancient religious retreat turned hotel, where you'll enjoy

---

Top left: Colorful fabrics boasting traditional patterns are plentiful in Cusco's markets.
Top middle: Bright feathered tropical birds perch on the grounds of the Inkaterra Machu Picchu Pueblo Hotel.
Top right: Maize for sale in Pisac market *Opposite:* A woman dressed in traditional clothing sells textiles in Chinchero.

the gardens, fountains, and pisco sours—or perhaps some coca leaf tea (one way to help your body acclimate to the altitude). You should also make sure to have a drink on one of the colonial-era balconies that overlook Cusco's stunning main square. Yes, the scene is touristy, but surveying it from above is incredibly romantic—almost as if you were in box seats at an old theater.

Once you're acclimated, walk the winding roads that lead up to the whitewashed San Blas neighborhood, a bohemian boutique mecca and a spectacular lookout point.

And when you're ready for the main event—your trip to Machu Picchu—take the Hiram Bingham, a swanky, old-school European train that's been dropped into the middle of the Andes and stocked with great food and drinks. But the best onboard offerings are the ever changing river and mountain views.

Another option is to spend a few days walking through the rain forests and ruins of the Inca Trail. Though you'll need to reserve at least a few months in advance to ensure permits and a guide, the effort is well worth your while. Beyond the beauty of the trek, there's a huge bonus: entering Machu Picchu before sunrise to experience the drama of daybreak over the mist-shrouded ruins—essentially by yourselves.

If hiking isn't for you, the next best thing is spending the night in the neighboring town of Aguas Calientes (see **Stay**) and boarding one of the morning's first buses, so you can get to Machu Picchu in time to beat the crowds and stake out your own secret spots among the stone structures and terraces. Another good reason to arrive early: There's a daily quota of people who can climb Huayna Picchu, the tallest peak at the site. Though the ascent isn't easy—one section will remind any *Princess Bride* fan of the Cliffs of Insanity—you'll be rewarded with sublime views of the river valley, the surrounding mountains, and, if you look closely, the red-petaled representations of the Inca princess's love.

Arrive at Machu Picchu early and you'll have the scenery and ruins to yourselves.

Opposite: Take a train for spectacular views and an early Machu Picchu arrival. *Above:* the Inkaterra Machu Picchu Pueblo Hotel

PLAN YOUR TRIP

STAY • Inkaterra Machu Picchu Pueblo Hotel, a National Geographic Unique Lodge, where you'll feel as if you're in a secret garden—or in a secret cloud forest. The hotel harbors hundreds of orchid, bird, and butterfly species and miles of trails, plus a smattering of cozy casitas and a welcoming riverside restaurant. Romantic extras include a twilight walk to a waterfall and candlelit sauna session for two in the spa's eucalyptus hut. *inkaterra.com*

EAT • Map Café, occupying the glassed-in patio of a beautiful old estate turned pre-Columbian art museum in Cusco. Among the renowned Novoandino specialties is the quinoa cannelloni with tomato, arugula, and goat cheese. *cuscorestaurants.com*

PLAY • Explore the Sacred Valley of the Inca, which begins just outside Cusco. The drive alone is worth the price of admission, but you should also make a few stops: Maras (surreal, sparkly salt pond terraces that cascade down a mountainside), Moray (mystical-feeling Inca crop circles), Chinchero (where a church built atop Inca ruins dominates the bucolic landscape), and Ollantaytambo (an impressive and climbable collection of Inca ruins). Habitats Peru can customize a Sacred Valley tour or any other romantic itinerary. *habitatsperu.com*

NEW YORK CITY

Celebrate Love in the Big Apple

One of the most recorded jazz standards of all time, "Autumn in New York," opens with a question about the city: "Why does it seem so inviting?" Composer Vernon Duke responds with various possibilities, from "glittering crowds and shimmering clouds" to "the promise of new love." And though his list is lovely (to hear it in its entirety, treat yourself to the Ella Fitzgerald version), he leaves out one very romantic fall detail: a whole city's worth of blazing red, orange, and yellow foliage. ✳ There are countless ways to savor the spectacle, but one of the most

romantic is taking a rowboat out for a spin around the leafy-looking glass that is the Central Park Lake. After basking in the reflected glory, order drinks and watch the golden hour set in at the lakeside Boathouse bar (open through October except in dodgy weather). Some other ridiculously romantic options: Cross the Brooklyn Bridge to the Brooklyn Heights Promenade, where the foliage is rivaled only by the views of Manhattan. Or take a stroll of a different kind along the High Line, a one-and-a-half-mile elevated park that's built along a former railroad track. Afterward, stop by Chelsea Market, the city's celebrated downtown food hall, for some truly exceptional culinary treats. And if you're visiting in early to mid-autumn, make your way to the Metropolitan Museum's Roof Garden Bar for Central Park panoramas that may well provide the best answer to Duke's question.

Top left: Walk the Brooklyn Bridge for cityscapes on both sides of the East River. *Top middle:* The king room at the Gramercy Park Hotel
Top right: Rent a rowboat in Central Park, then enjoy cocktails and appetizers at the Boathouse.

The concrete jungle certainly gets a healthy—and beautiful—dose of color come autumn.

PLAN YOUR TRIP

STAY • Gramercy Park Hotel, where you'll get a highly coveted key to the adjacent private park, a sweet little haven for artists, authors, and musicians since the 19th century. The hotel, which has hosted everyone from JFK to Blondie to Bono, is as cozy a retreat as you'll find in the city, with roaring fireplaces, oak floors, tapestry chairs, and stunning park views.

EAT • One If by Land, Two If by Sea, which occupies Aaron Burr's 1767 carriage house. Here the brick fireplaces, candlelit tables, private garden, and baby grand conspire to produce one of the highest engagement rates in the city. Try the famed beef Wellington, but leave room for a (perhaps ring-revealing) dessert. *oneifbyland.com*

PLAY • Couples are contractually obliged to go to the top of the Empire State Building, scene of some of the most iconic romantic movie moments ever (*Love Affair, Affair to Remember, Sleepless in Seattle*)—and contrary to popular opinion, you *can* have a crowd-free experience here. Given that the observatory is open until 2 a.m., head up after midnight (the last elevator to the top leaves at 1:15 a.m.). Chances are you'll have the place—and those stunning nighttime views—to yourselves. *esbnyc.com*

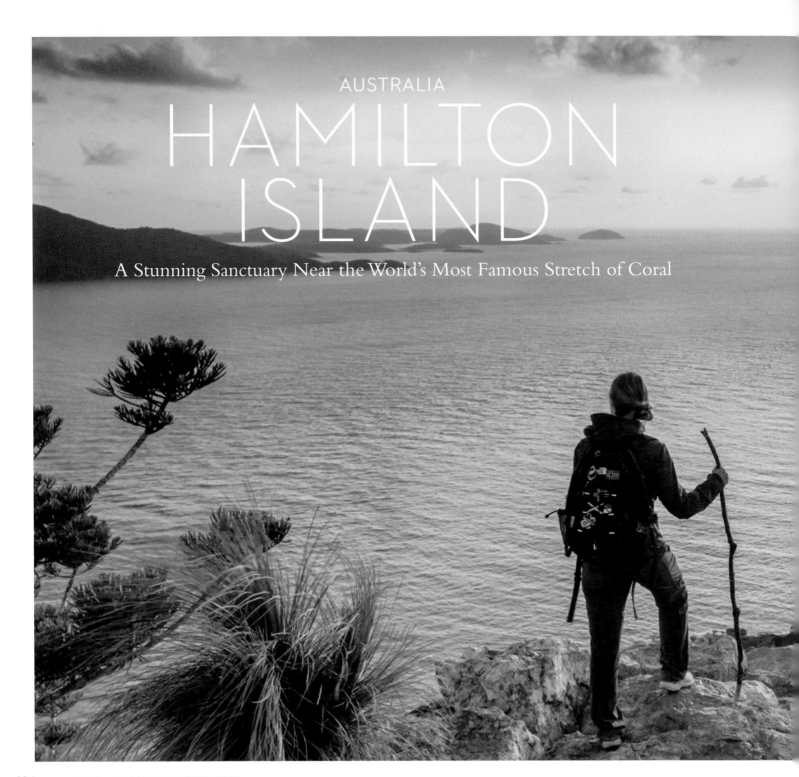

AUSTRALIA

HAMILTON ISLAND

A Stunning Sanctuary Near the World's Most Famous Stretch of Coral

Take in the panoramic views of Queensland from Hamilton Island at sunrise.

Positioned at the gateway to the Great Barrier Reef, Hamilton Island puts out a special welcome mat for romantics: a natural heart-shaped coral reef. Aptly named Heart Reef and sitting about 20 minutes offshore, it's easily mistaken for a mirage—even after you circle it a couple of times in the air (see **Play**). * And as you'll quickly learn, that gorgeous heart is hardly the exception around here. Hamilton is all about natural beauty, so much so that the island is virtually car free, with the exception of a few shuttles. Renting a buggy—similar to a golf cart—is one fun way to get around. But you'll want to walk as much as possible. The hills are blanketed

in lush greenery and laced with trails that lead to secluded coves, ancient groves—and, in the case of Passage Peak (the highest point on the island), unsurpassed views of the Coral Sea and Whitsunday Islands.

Mind you, some of the best hikes here take you not up but down. The Escape Beach Trail, for example, leads you past a

wildlife-rich mangrove to the clear waters of the trail's namesake beach, one of several secluded coves on the island. Or take the slightly more challenging trail to Coral Cove, a quiet beach with southern views all the way to Linderman Island.

On less isolated beaches, you'll find all kinds of watercraft for two—and indeed, kayaking or catamaraning around the not

Floor-to-ceiling, wall-to-wall windows make every spot from your room in the Qualia's Windward Pavilion a winner.

quite two-square-mile island is among the most beautiful ways to experience it.

Of course, what lies below the surface is beautiful, too. One of the best places to take a peek is the nearby Reefworld, a pontoon above the Hardy Reef section of the Great Barrier Reef. Among the coral's countless colorful residents—which includes clown fish, unicornfish, angelfish, and butterflyfish, to name a few—is the endearingly bizarre Maori wrasse, whose neon-veined head hump makes the poor thing look like he's always *just* bumped into something.

Though leaving this water world behind is tough, reef-top massages on the pontoon give you plenty of reason to surface. For the ultimate in reef romance, however, spend the night on the pontoon. Book a Reefworld "Reefsleep," and you'll camp out in bedrolls under the stars. The experience includes evening cocktails, a barbecue dinner, stargazing, and—if you're certified—a night dive. And while the music of the ocean waves can make for particularly sound sleep, *do not* miss sunrise over the Great Barrier Reef, when the ordinarily aqua surface often goes through a flaming fuchsia phase.

Sunsets are equally impressive in this part of the world, and there's a long-standing tradition of celebrating them on Hamilton. Once late afternoon rolls around, you'll want to walk, take a buggy, or shuttle to the One Tree Hill lookout.

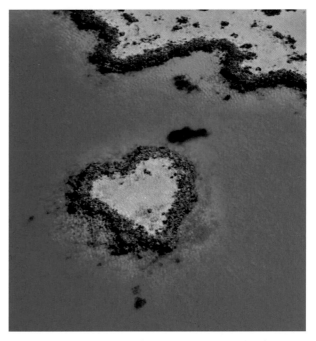

What's more romantic than a heart-shaped coral reef?

Here, you'll find a menu of sunset cocktails at a tiny bar, as well as benches that position you perfectly for one of nature's most romantic shows.

PLAN YOUR TRIP

STAY • Qualia, a series of airy pavilions—all timber, stone, and glass—tucked into the dense tropical greenery of Hamilton's secluded northern tip. Any space here comes with breathtaking water views, but the Leeward Pavilions are designed for optimal sunset spectating, and the Windward Pavilions have infinity pools that seem to dissolve into the Coral Sea. At the legendary spa, try the Sweet Moments couples treatment: a mocha-infused milk bath followed by a chocolate-spice rubdown that includes the signature drifting scalp massage and grounding foot massage. *qualia.com.au*

EAT • Bommie, short for the indigenous word *bombora* (loose translation: "waves that break in the shallows"), and when you have sunset drinks on the prow-like deck that extends into the marina, the name will make perfect sense. Once the sun drops, retreat to the dining room for some of the most raved-about food on the island, such as the marinated yellowfin tuna with rockmelon, seaweed, and cashews—plus glittering water views through floor-to-ceiling windows. *hamiltonisland.com.au*

PLAY • Take a helicopter ride over Heart Reef. Then have a private picnic on nearby Whitehaven Beach—another local legend, thanks to countless hallucinatory swirls of impossibly white sand and aqua sea—before your chopper returns to whisk you home. *hamiltonislandair.com*

A horse-drawn sleigh glides through the snow-covered countryside of Sils, Switzerland.

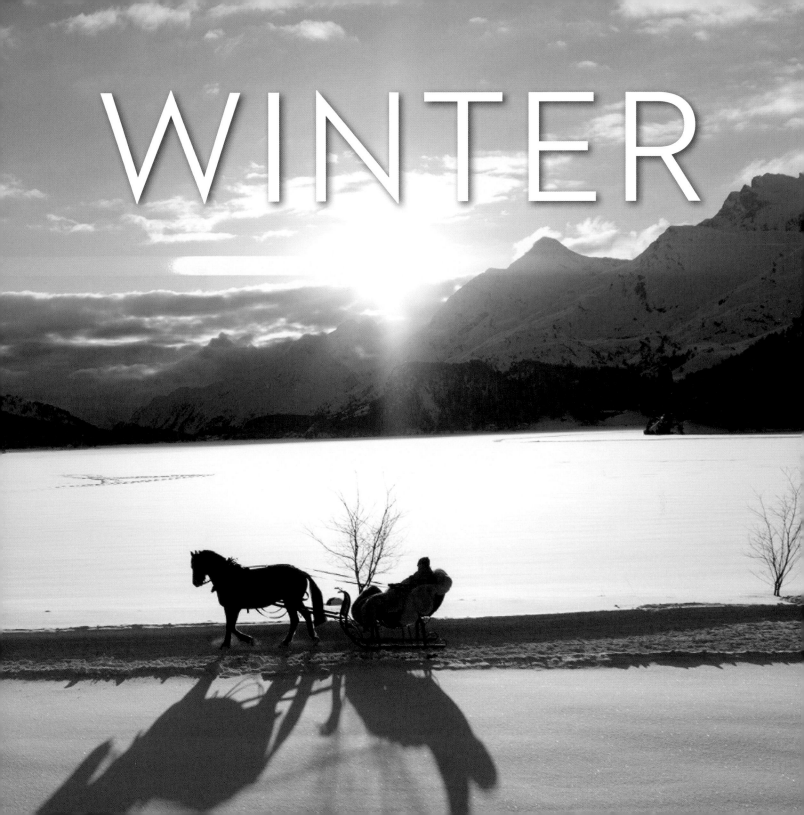

WINTER

SOUTH ISLAND

An Over-the-Top Adventure at the Bottom of the World

Award-winning vineyards
in the Marlborough
district of South Island

New Zealand is a nation of extremes. Extreme sports (including, most famously, commercial bungee jumping) are said to have been born here, turning Queenstown into the self-styled Adventure Capital of the World. Then there's the extreme beauty of the place, and particularly the South Island, where you'll find everything from the sparkling Southern Alps to hilly seaside vineyards to cascade-filled fjords. So for couples, the math is pretty simple: Extreme adventure plus extreme beauty equals extreme romance. * Begin at the beginning: the 1880 suspension bridge that gave the world commercial bungee jumping and still provides your only

opportunity to take a tandem leap in Queenstown. Spanning a dramatic river gorge, the Kawarau Bridge was once a gold-mining thoroughfare but now serves exclusively as a jumping-off point for this 141-foot plunge.

For a completely different kind of extreme romance, book an Over the Top helicopter to fly you through the diamantine Southern Alps with a stop for a secluded picnic en route to the glacier-carved Milford Sound.

You'll also want to see this waterfall-streaked fjord—the Eighth Wonder of the World, by Rudyard Kipling's estimation—on a day cruise or a tandem kayak. Or, if you lean superadventurous, scuba dive your way through. Below the dark, still surface, you'll find the dazzling array of coral trees, fish, octopuses, sharks, and dolphins that inspired Jacques Cousteau to declare the Fjordland one of his favorite dive sites of all time.

Gorgeous lupine flowers pepper the mountain tops bordering Lake Wakatipu and Queenstown.

Another South Island variation on adventure romance? Cycle one of at least five vineyard trails: Central Otago, a Pinot Noir paradise; Marlborough, home to legendary Sauvignon Blancs; and Canterbury, Nelson, and the Waipara Valley, all producers of delicate off-dry whites.

To give yourselves a breather between adventures, try the unofficial national pastime, and campervan your way through the countryside for a couple days. Tricked-out vehicles outfitted with linens, cookware, and more are plentiful here—you can't miss the purple and green Juicy ones on the road—so you can basically grab the keys and go. And given that 10 out of New Zealand's 14 national parks are located on the South Island, there's no shortage of routes to choose from.

But you can't go wrong if you head for Nelson. This sunny city by the Tasman Bay blends 19th-century colonial vestiges with thoroughly modern surprises (the World of WearableArt and Classic Cars Museum, for example, has become a global phenomenon). Nelson has another big draw, however: proximity to 3 of those 10 South Island national parks—the most beloved being Abel Tasman. Hike and kayak through the golden beaches and turquoise waters of New Zealand's only coastal national park and you may well be ruined for all other road trips.

While you're in the neighborhood, visit Jens Hansen, the jeweler who designed the "One Ring" for the New

The flower-covered entrance to Blanket Bay's chalet

Zealand–filmed *Hobbit* and *Lord of the Rings* series. Though you may not want an exact replica of "my precious," you'll surely find something that's equally beautiful—in the extreme.

PLAN YOUR TRIP

STAY • Blanket Bay, tucked between sparkling Lake Wakatipu and the peaks of the Humboldt Mountains—with outsize windows for gazing at both. Your drive to the resort will be one of the most beautiful you'll ever make, with a dramatic new view around almost every turn. And whether or not you sign on for the official honeymoon package, arrange for a candlelit dinner in the wine cave. *blanketbay.com*

EAT • Stratosfare Restaurant & Bar, perched almost 1,500 feet above Queenstown at the top of the Skyline Gondola track (the views of the city, Lake Wakatipu, and the mountains are especially breathtaking from your table at sunset). Local specialties include the Akaroa salmon and wild Fjordland venison steaks. *skyline.co.nz/queenstown/restaurant*

PLAY • Hike across (and into) the amazing seven-and-a-half-mile-long Franz Josef Glacier. Then take a dip in the steaming, rain forest–shrouded Glacier Hot Pools, a series of six natural hot springs that have their own romantic backstory. According to Maori legend, the pools are fed by the tears of Kā Roimata o Hinehukatere, who's pining for her lost true love. *glacierhotpools.co.nz*

THE GOLDEN TRIANGLE

Monumental Testaments to Love and Beauty

Perhaps the most fabled triple-header in travel—the circuit linking Delhi, Agra, and Jaipur—overflows with romance. But the triumvirate's pièce de résistance is the Taj Mahal in Agra, history's greatest architectural ode to love. This marble megamausoleum was commissioned by the heartbroken 17th-century Mogul emperor Shah Jahan after his favorite wife, Mumtaz Mahal, died while delivering their 14th child. Romance seekers should consider it their first stop. * By some estimates, 22,000 artisans and 1,000 elephants took more than 22 years to perfect what the Bengali poet Rabindranath Tagore called this "teardrop on the face of eternity." And though the impulse may be to simply lose yourselves among the resulting archways, columns,

and courtyards, there's so much romantic lore here— and so many insider secrets—you should consider taking a private tour (see **Play**). If you can swing the timing, go during the full moon, when the mausoleum's silhouette goes from merely magnificent to thoroughly mystical.

Nearby you'll find the 17th-century red sandstone Agra Fort, whose beauty belies the building's role in Shah Jahan's

---

Top left: Thousands of dancers perform in the old part of the Pink City (Jaipur) to celebrate a festival. *Top middle:* Piles of colorful Holi powder
Top right: A rickshaw passes the Hawa Mahal monument in Jaipur. *Opposite:* Chandra Mahal, or the City Palace

romantic narrative: He was put under house arrest here by a son who declared him unfit to rule not long after the Taj Mahal was completed.

Delhi, a three-hour drive from Agra, has a Red Fort as well, and you won't want to miss this hulking remnant of the Mogul architectural golden age. Other local must-sees include the 17th-century Jama Masjid (one of India's largest mosques) and Humayan's tomb, a 16th-century Persian-Mogul hybrid mausoleum that seems to float above the surrounding gardens.

But one Delhi highlight is specific to this season. The Qutub Festival is a local classical music extravaganza at the Qutb Minar complex, where you'll find the tallest brick minaret on Earth. (Though the dates vary they often fall in late November and early December.)

A little more than four hours from Delhi sits Jaipur, known as the Pink City, thanks to the rosy stone that makes up the oldest part of town. And this is the place to palace hop. Consider the 1799 Hawa Mahal, or Palace of the Winds, with its tapering, almost cake-like rows of windows and screens. Or the sprawling, ornate mishmash of styles and eras that is the City Palace, still occupied in part by royals. Or the 16th-century Amer (or Amber) Fort and Palace—a stunning hilltop study in red sandstone and marble that overlooks Maota Lake.

Jaipur is also renowned for its buzzing bazaars, where exquisite textiles and jewels are so dangerously abundant, you may wind up needing an extra suitcase. Check out the block-print, tie-dyed, and embroidered fabrics of Bapu Bazaar—and, for jewelry, the Johnri and Chameliwala Bazaars. The tangled alleys of the latter house a particularly astonishing selection of gems, so while you may never have a Taj Mahal built in your honor (21st-century building codes can be *so* restrictive), the area may still inspire your partner to make a monumental statement of love. Time will tell!

You'll feel like royalty poolside at the Oberoi Amarvilas hotel in Agra.

Opposite: A young man and elephant at the Amer (Amber) Fort in Jaipur *Above:* The Taj Mahal is the world's most romantic building.

PLAN YOUR TRIP

STAY • The Oberoi Amarvilas, less than half a mile from the Taj Mahal, has guest rooms that look out onto the celebrated site. Given the view, take advantage of one of the hotel's most romantic offerings: a candlelit, flower-bedecked dinner for two on your own balcony. Even the spa treatment rooms have a view of those iconic white domes. Not that the hotel's romance is linked exclusively to the Taj Mahal: You'll find beautiful terraced lawns, reflection pools, pavilions, and a sparkling, chandelier-lit lounge. Perhaps most romantic of all is the couples blessing ceremony (complete with an exchange of garlands). *oberoihotels.com*

EAT • Dum Pukht is widely considered one of the best restaurants in Asia, if not on Earth. A rhapsody in blue (and silver, and crystal, and scalloped archways), this sumptuous space in New Delhi is a nod to 18th- and 19th-century Nawab (the state now known as Uttar Pradesh) and the local tradition of cooking over a slow fire in sealed earthenware with subtle spices and delicate flavoring. *itchotels.in*

PLAY • Book one of Viator's private tours of the Taj Mahal—as much for the line-cutting access as for the guide's insider intel on the calligraphy, inlays, history, and more. *viator.com*

ST. MORITZ

Romantic Hikes, Après-Ski Treats, and Glittering Mountain Peaks

Perhaps not surprising for a place that boasts Europe's highest-altitude casino, modern St. Moritz began with a wager. As the story goes, the town's first hotelier made an offer to his last guests of the 1864 summer season: Come back in winter, and if you don't enjoy yourselves, you'll be reimbursed. So they returned at Christmas—and didn't leave until spring. Thus Alpine winter tourism was born. ✳ You'll be thrilled that it was—especially if you roll into town on the Bernina or Glacier Express trains, the best way to get here.

A romantic world unto themselves, they pick you up at a Swiss or Italian hub and whisk you through white, glittering Alpine landscapes until you reach the even more glittering St. Moritz.

Yes, this celebrated resort is a Cristal magnum and Chanel moon boot kind of a place. But the bling blends right into the backdrop: the brilliant slopes of the Engadin Valley, home to 58 ski lifts, 217 miles of runs—and one especially romantic hike. A mix of natural and man-made beauty, the Muottas Muragl Philosophers' Trail is lined with plaques that bear inspiring quotations from such greats as Socrates and Sartre. Along the way, you'll find both stunning panoramas and blanket-draped benches to snuggle on. Warm up inside with hot chocolate at the nearby and aptly named Romantik Hotel Muottas Muragl.

Top left: Badrutt's Palace lights up snowy St. Moritz. *Top middle:* The inviting Renaissance Bar in Badrutt's Palace offers whiskey and cigars any time of day. *Top right:* More than 70 trails await skiers who visit St. Moritz.

The Glacier Express winds its way through the Alps' snowy landscape.

PLAN YOUR TRIP

STAY • Badrutt's Palace, a fixture on the St. Moritz scene since 1896. This lakeside spread with amazing Alpine vistas has long been a favorite of royals and celebs—most notably, Alfred Hitchcock, who is said to have returned 34 times after honeymooning here. Book a Beau Rivage Suite and you'll get the most magical mountain views—especially from your marble tub. *badruttspalace.com*

EAT • El Paradiso, about 7,000 feet up the Corviglia slopes. Enjoy the spectacular views, sheepskin-covered outdoor seating, and candelabra-bedecked alfresco bar, along with one of the best wine lists in the Alps. Don't miss the fondue or sweet pancakes with caramelized apples. And when you've gorged on all the food you can handle, either ski down or walk 10 minutes to the Suvretta lift to descend. *el-paradiso.ch*

PLAY • Soak up some warmth. After skiing, hiking, eating, and drinking your way through the Engadin's slopes, you'll be ready for some steamy thermal waters. Enter the Mineral Bath and Spa Samedan, a complex built improbably in a landmark-protected church in the nearby historic village of Samedan. *mineralbad-samedan.ch*

MALDIVES

Your Own Private Patch of Island Paradise

Meet some one percenters you can't help but love: the Maldivian isles. Because 99 percent of the Republic of the Maldives is water (specifically, the Indian Ocean), the remaining one percent (i.e., the land) tends to feel extremely intimate and secluded. And those two attributes happen to go very well with romance. ✳ Yes, this archipelago that sits 270 miles south of India is the sort of place you visit when you *really* want to feel marooned together, with off-campus activities limited—by definition—to the water. You may be able to visit a local village if there's another island nearby—and just watching the local fishermen ply the Indian Ocean in

their *dhonis*—traditional Maldivian boats with the most gracefully upturned noses—will be worth the trip.

But the islands' main attraction, of course, is closer to home: the 50 shades of blue just outside your room, along with the 350 coral species and thousands of fish that come with the package. In fact, the average house reef is so vibrant you don't even need to jump on a dive boat to be awed; you can basically roll out of bed and into a Jacques Cousteau special. When you're back on land, expect a full schedule of pool plunging, daybed lounging, and spa going. Plus the kind of canoodling that happens only on a secluded island (or a chain of 1,190 of them).

Top left: You can snorkel right off your bungalow in the tropical lagoons of the Maldives. *Top middle:* Undersea creatures, like the nodule sea star, decorate the ocean's floors. *Top right:* Board a traditional dhoni from the banks of the Kuramathi Island Resort for a sunset cruise.

The sanctuaries at Jumeirah Dhevanafushi include private pools overlooking the ocean.

PLAN YOUR TRIP

STAY • Jumeirah Dhevanafushi, where you'll have a luxe overwater suite or private patch of shore from which to take in the infinite water views. You'll also enjoy the scenery when you're facedown on the massage table at the overwater Talise spa. Watch in amazement as eels, sharks, and massive schools of tropical fish swim under you. There's also an overwater gym where you can work up an appetite for the private island feast that the hotel will be happy to arrange. *jumeirah.com*

EAT • Though you'll do the majority of your eating wherever you're staying (almost every resort occupies a private island, so restaurant hopping is tough), you may well spend a bit of time in Male—either because of your international flight timing or because you want to see the country's capital. Either way, eat at Azur restaurant, atop Hotel Jen Male. You'll get panoramic sea views, fresh fusion cuisine, and welcome breezes. *hoteljen.com*

PLAY • Given the warmth of this patch of Indian Ocean, you're in the perfect place to try a new water sport—say, kitesurfing. Or wakeboarding. After all, you're hardly going to mind falling in while you learn.

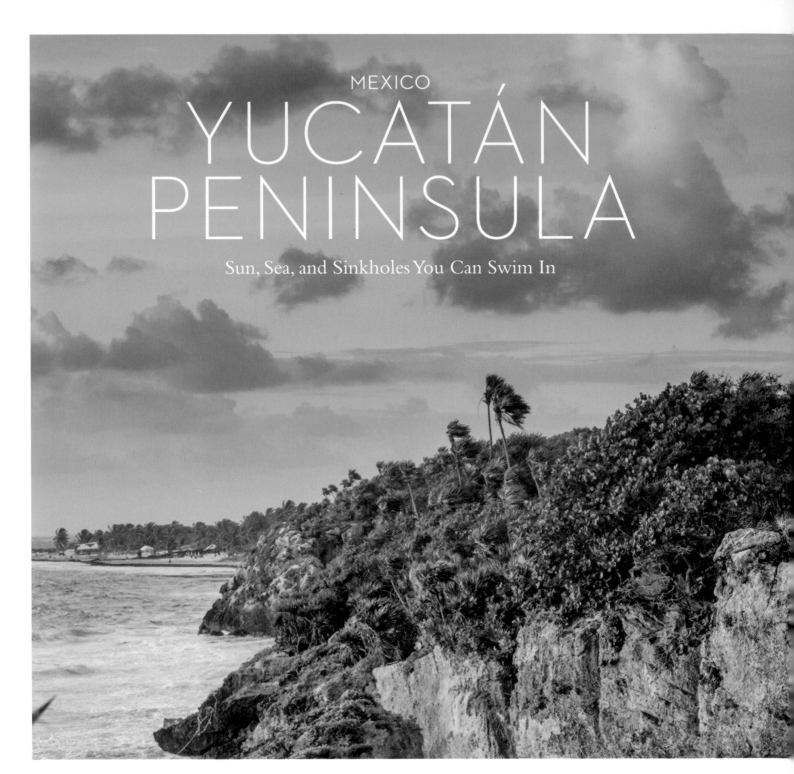

MEXICO

YUCATÁN PENINSULA

Sun, Sea, and Sinkholes You Can Swim In

Tulum ruins, including the Maya Castillo, adorn the Yucatán Peninsula.

You can search high and low for romance here—and you'll find it in either case. From soaring Maya ruins to subterranean swimming holes, what awaits you on this gorgeous peninsula between the Gulf of Mexico and the Caribbean is an otherworldly adventure for two. * In fact, there are so many hauntingly beautiful remains of the Maya heyday that you could easily spend your entire trip exploring them. But your short list should include Chichén Itzá, among the largest and most politically and economically important Maya cities; Cobá, home to the peninsula's tallest Maya pyramid, where a spectacular jungle panorama awaits; and Tulum, one of a few

walled Maya cities, with stunning, cliff-top sea views. This last site is particularly beloved, given that you can interrupt your tour of the ruins at any point to scurry down a cliff and jump in the turquoise sea. Once you're refreshed, put your clothes back on, hike back up, and continue wandering in awe around the palace, the frescoed temple, and El Castillo.

There's the Maya underworld to consider as well, and though you probably wouldn't want to go all the way in (it's the local equivalent of Hades), visiting its gateways is one of the most popular local pursuits. Known locally as cenotes, these limestone sinkholes—often filled with transparent blue-green water and surrounded by lush

Ik-Kil Cenote, near Chichén Itzá, is just one of many sinkholes you can swim in around the peninsula.

greenery—are a trademark of the region. In fact, Chichén Itzá takes its name (loose translation: "at the mouth of the well") from a resident cenote. That one isn't swimmable, but you'll find plenty along the peninsula that are, and some can even be dived.

There are countless other places to explore the local nature, too. One of the best is the Sian Ka'an Biosphere Reserve, home to hundreds of species of birds, reptiles, fish, and mammals (this is a great place to spot a manatee). Spend a day hiking or boating here—or boat through the mangroves of Celestun, a 147,500-acre national park that serves as the winter home to flamingos, herons, and pelicans, as well as the hatching ground for endangered sea turtles.

However beautiful the local nature, it's occasionally rivaled by an urban landscape—Mérida being a prime example. The peninsula's post-*conquista* cultural capital, the city is filled with museums, theaters, churches, plazas, parks, and haciendas. It's the perfect place to spend a day—or night. Specifically, Thursday night, when you can watch the *serenatas Yucatecas* (Yucatecan serenades) that take place in the colonial arcade-edged Parque Santa Lucía. Also on the square: Apoala, a beloved local hangout with Oaxacan-inspired food and a romantic terrace.

For a completely different kind of city experience, hit the quintessential beach town of Playa del Carmen,

A couple in traditional dress dance at a fiesta.

where the main draws are sun, sand, and surf. And after all the trip's ascents and descents, a couple of sea-level loungers, with a side of margaritas, will be just what the shaman ordered.

PLAN YOUR TRIP

STAY • Rosewood Mayakoba, part of a canal- and lagoon-filled complex on the Riviera Maya where you get around as much by boat as on foot. Arguably the most romantic rooms here are the overwater lagoon suites, complete with outdoor rain showers, plunge pools, and private docks. If you book the couples Eclipse Sun & Moon Journey, a boat will pick you up from your dock and whisk you off to the private island spa. On the menu: a scrub and wrap of cacao and rose petals, followed by an unforgettable massage. *rosewoodhotels.com*

EAT • Aldea Corazón, a foodie's Eden hiding in plain sight. Behind a nondescript entrance on Playa del Carmen's Quinta Avenida sits a leafy, torchlit secret garden, complete with cenote and waterfall. There's also a great local menu with imaginative twists: mezcal-flambéed *queso fundido*, for example. *grupoazotea.com*

PLAY • Visit Isla Holbox, an island of tranquillity at the peninsula's northeastern tip in the Yum Balam ecological reserve. On this cute little car-free combo of mangrove and beach, you can swim, snorkel, kiteboard—or simply chill.

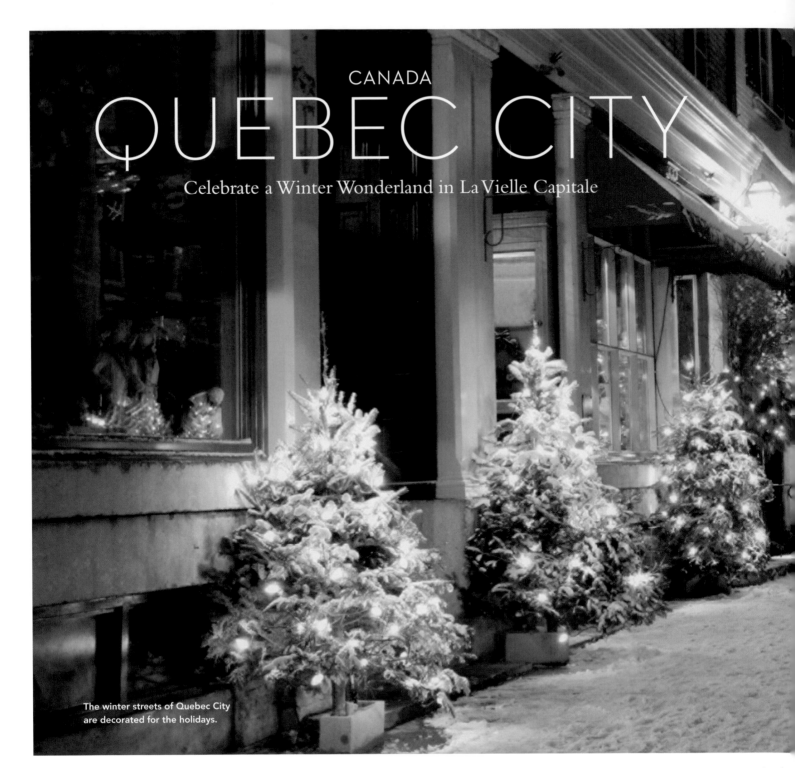

CANADA

QUEBEC CITY

Celebrate a Winter Wonderland in La Vielle Capitale

The winter streets of Quebec City
are decorated for the holidays.

Long before *Frozen* became a cultural phenomenon, French Canadians were on to the secret: No one is immune to the seductions of a proper winter wonderland. Indeed, Arendelle was still decades away from its Disney debut when Quebec City introduced an ice palace for a centerpiece, jingling sleighs for transport, and a chummy snowman for a mascot. And to this day, La Vielle Capitale serves up a frozen fairy tale of cinematic proportions. ✳ For the full effect, plan your trip during Carnaval de Québec, a 19th-century tradition now reprised annually. Lording over the festivities is the spokes-snowman, Bonhomme, a seven-foot-tall

reincarnation of a character every Quebecer knows and loves from childhood. In late January, the mayor gives him the keys to the city, and for the next couple of weeks, the gentle giant rules from an ice palace opposite Parliament. In fact, you can tour his digs at prescribed times during the festival if you'd like.

Whether as spectators or participants, you'll want to catch the canoe races across the frozen St. Lawrence River, the music- and float-filled night parades, the winter symphony, the international snow sculpture competition, the sleigh rides, and the dogsledding. Hard-core winter lovers will also want to try the snow bath (a group romp through the powder with nothing more than bathing suits and boots for warmth). Whether you go for a snow bath or

The Fairmont Le Château Frontenac towers over the city's skyline with its colorful exterior.

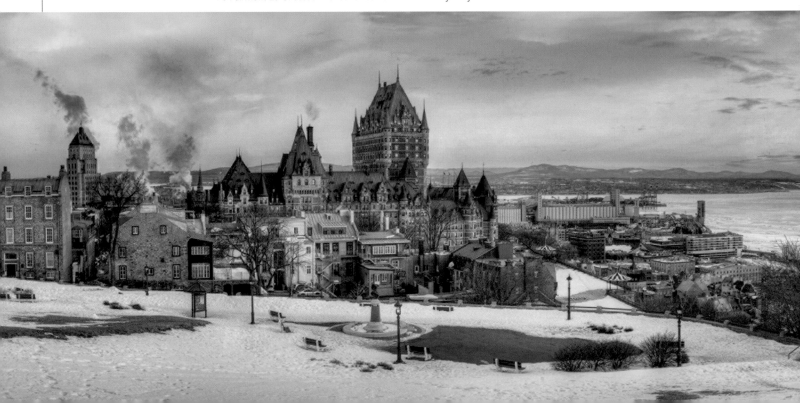

not, you'll quickly adopt the best local trick to getting toasty: Snuggle up and drink copious amounts of caribou, the hot Québécois wine that's toted in hollowed-out canes—each traditionally capped with the head of Bonhomme. The festival also heralds the arrival of a sugar shack (home to all things maple syrup), outdoor ice bars (try ice wine or ice cider), and a city-wide Poutine Week (a celebration of the local blend of french fries, cheese curds, and gravy).

But even if you don't come for Carnaval, winter is still very much a wonderland here, as you'll see when you walk the suspension bridge over Montmorency Falls. The cascade is almost 100 feet taller than Niagara Falls and freezes into fantastical formations—some of which look more like stalagmites than ice. And the aesthetic is only part of the romance: When a beautiful 18th-century Québécois bride-to-be learned that her intended had died in battle, she reportedly donned her wedding gown and threw herself into the falls— and the locals (who have come to view the area as a lovers' lane of sorts) say you can see her through the mists.

Two more traditional stops on the winter courtship circuit: the outdoor ice-skating rink in Place d'Youville, across from a gate to the Old Quebec ramparts, and the Toboggan Slide Au 1884, a 19th-century icon that'll send you hurtling

The deluxe guest room at the Fairmont Le Château Frontenac

down a track together at almost 45 miles an hour. And if by chance you do feel a chill, repeat the mantra that went triple platinum and won an Oscar and a Grammy in the process: "The cold never bothered me anyway."

PLAN YOUR TRIP

STAY • Fairmont Le Château Frontenac, the iconic castle-style hotel overlooking the St. Lawrence River. You could easily spend your whole trip cozied up by the fireplace at the hotel's 1608 Wine & Cheese Bar. But during a flurry, head straight for the hot tub in the sixth-floor solarium. Watching the flakes fall as the steam rises from the old city's rooftops is the picture of storybook romance (if storybooks had hot tubs, of course). *fairmont.com*

EAT • Panache, a two-story, dimly lit old warehouse with exposed wooden beams, stone walls, the cushiest possible seating, a glass-enclosed central fireplace—and a chef who earned his stripes at a succession of Michelin-starred restaurants across the Pond. Whatever you order, leave room for dessert. The amazing caramel mille-feuille comes with three scoops of vanilla ice cream: one infused with Tahitian vanilla, one

with Mexican, and one with Malagasy. *saint-antoine.com*

PLAY • Check out the local ice hotel, or Hôtel de Glace, as day-trippers. You can buy a pass that lets you tour the guest rooms (overnighters don't have exclusive access until dark) and public spaces. Don't miss the various ice bars, ice chapel, and indoor ice slide. *hoteldeglace-canada.com*

THE CARIBBEAN

White Sands, Azure Sea, and Volcanic Peaks

Find beauty overlooking Gustavia Harbour's boats, candy-colored roofs, and turquoise sea.

"Caribbean reality," mused the famed novelist and journalist Gabriel García Márquez, "resembles the wildest imagination." Thus the wall-less hotel on page 226. And the candy-colored downtown on the page after that. And any number of dreamlike discoveries you'll make during your own explorations of these glorious islands. But of all local offerings, the best may well be the simplest: the pristine beach that you have to yourselves; the warm current that transects your snorkel path; the hibiscus blossoms that bejewel your pillows; and the hospitality that makes you feel at home in this alternate reality.

Set sail into the aquamarine sea off the coast of St. Barth.

ST. BARTHÉLEMY

Not until 1957, when David Rockefeller bought a property on this exquisite island—named after Christopher Columbus's brother Bartholomew in 1493—did St. Barth take on the identity the world knows today. Jet-setters soon followed the famed banker, all enchanted by the magical topography, and the little Leeward hideaway became the Caribbean *it* isle, with its heady blend of glamour and beauty (think serene mountain peaks, richly varied vegetation, and an embarrassment of perfect beaches).

Even with the variety of posh local haunts, those pristine beaches are the real defining characteristic of the island. Colombier, hugged by a forested semicircle and filled with tranquil water, is arguably the most romantic; the only way to get here is by boat or footpaths. Then there's Corossol, beloved for its traditional fishing boats. And Marigot, home to stellar snorkeling. The list goes on, but no matter where you roam on any given day, you should eventually make your way to Shell Beach, where the sunsets are legend. Settle in with a couple of cocktails at Do Brazil to see why.

PLAN YOUR TRIP

STAY Cheval Blanc, on the wide—and widely adored—Baie des Flamands. The house decor, stark and serene (*right*), is offset by colorful tropical gardens, where an open-air couples massage tops the romantic to-do list. Also be sure to book a fancy French picnic on a nearby desert island. *stbarthisledefrance.chevalblanc.com*

Caribbean features decorate the garden bungalow at the Cheval Blanc Hotel.

Private infinity pools in the rooms of the Jade Mountain resort offer the best views of the Pitons.

ST. LUCIA

"I come from a place that likes grandeur," wrote the Nobel-winning poet and playwright Derek Walcott. And before you even touch down on his home turf, you'll see his point. Actually, you'll see two of them: the Pitons (*left*). A World Heritage site and the island's calling card, these fraternal twin peaks are all drama, their forested slopes rising straight out of the sea and tapering precipitously toward the sky.

Chances are you'll want to commune with this dramatic duo early and often, and opportunities abound. Consider hiking the Gros Piton for the gorgeous challenge of it—and for the panorama that you'll find up top. Or view the Petit Piton from a zip line that also whisks you over a plantation's worth of cocoa, coffee, mango, and palm trees.

Another hugely popular option? Tour the geothermal field in the Pitons World Heritage site. Dubbed a drive-in volcano, this crater is home to countless fumaroles, bubbling mud pools, and sulfur-spewing springs. You can even bathe in certain sulfur pools. Yes, the aroma takes some getting used to, but once you're immersed together—and the mineral's soothing properties start to kick in—you'll find youselves wanting to settle in for a while. Especially given the dramatic surroundings.

But perhaps the best way to enjoy the Pitons is with a snorkel and mask. If you take a boat to the mountains' base, you'll find that the local undersea world is, in the words of Walcott, a place that likes grandeur.

PLAN YOUR TRIP

STAY Jade Mountain resort, designed by celebrated architect Nicholas Troubetzkoy. The guest rooms (aptly called sanctuaries) are cut into a cliff side and have no outer wall, so there's nothing between you and your Pitons panorama. Marvel at the scene from the sumptuous, mosquito-netted bed, elegant sun loungers, or your private infinity pool. The food is also exquisite here. *jademountain.com*

Traditional multicolored town houses and outdoor restaurants decorate the waterfront in Curaçao.

CURAÇAO

There's almost no feature of Curaçao that doesn't seem like a waking dream—beginning with the capital. The Handelskade's waterfront (*above*) is filled with 17th-century Dutch architecture that's been transformed by bright candy colors. Then there's the Queen Emma Pontoon Bridge, which swings open when big ships need to pass. Given that it's the entertainment throughout the day, you may want to stake out a table at one of the cafés that face the floating bridge so you can enjoy the spectacle with cocktails in hand.

But Curaçao is the kind of place where you'll spend as much time below the surface as above—and things get even more hallucinatory underwater, not least at the magic Mushroom Forest, one of 65 or so dive sites here. Each offers a different spectacle: outsize pillar corals, polka-dot octopuses, and fish that match every one of the candy-colored buildings on land.

PLAN YOUR TRIP

STAY Kura Hulanda Lodge & Beach Club, a cliff-top hideaway that overlooks a swath of teeming turquoise. The lodge borders one of Curaçao's most beloved dive sites: the aptly named Alice in Wonderland, where green moray eels, lobsters, star coral, and a whole variety of vibrant fish await. *kurahulanda.com*

ST. VINCENT AND THE GRENADINES

If St. Barth is built for beach hopping, St. Vincent and the Grenadines is built for island hopping. Make Petit St. Vincent your home base, and the house motorboat fleet will happily transport you to any of a number of renowned neighbors (see **Stay**).

First, head to the Tobago Cays, a cluster of tiny jewels set in an ethereal aqua wildlife reserve (read: fabulous snorkeling). Then there's Carriacou, where you can check out the boat-building traditions of Windward Village—or sample the legendary pizza at the Lazy Turtle. At the other end of the spectrum is Mustique, where palatial villas dot the coast (have a drink at Basil's Bar, where you may well run into Mick Jagger or Kate Middleton). For golfers, there's Canouan, with its stunning 18-hole course. And for guaranteed smiles (and really good drinks), there's the one and only conch shell isle known as Happy Island.

PLAN YOUR TRIP

STAY Petit St. Vincent, a National Geographic Unique Lodge where you'll find spectacular views, gifted spa therapists, and a beloved semaphore system that's used in place of phones. A mini-flagpole of sorts sits outside your cottage and communicates your every desire to the staff. Need your favorite drinks delivered to your hammock? Raise the yellow flag. Then need some privacy? Raise the red flag. *petitstvincent.com*

You may just find yourselves snorkeling with sea turtles as your swimming partner in the Tobago Cays.

GERMANY
ROMANTIC ROAD

Holiday Markets, Dreamy Castles, and Steamy Mulled Wine

Welcome to fairy tale central. Not far from Hessen—home turf of the Brothers Grimm—sits the landmark that inspired Disney's Sleeping Beauty Castle: Neuschwanstein (see page 234), the 19th-century home of Ludwig the Fairy Tale King, a famously reclusive dreamer. And you'd be hard-pressed to find a more appropriate starting point on the Romantic Road. As you look out over the river gorge and forests of the Hohenschwangau Valley from the king's secluded hilltop in the Bavarian Alps, steal your own version of Princess Aurora's "love's first kiss" to inaugurate the trip. * Spanning 200 miles between the

states of Bavaria and Baden-Württemberg, the fabled Romantic Road is a grand tour of castles, medieval towns, Alpine backdrops, and, in winter, Christmas markets. In fact, the markets alone—with their hot mulled wine, twinkling lights, roving singers, and required snuggling—

are a huge romantic draw. And all that sparkly snow doesn't hurt either.

After touring the opulent grounds of Neuschwanstein and being regaled with tales of King Ludwig's eccentricities, you'll want to visit the nearby Hohenschwangau and Linderhof to

---

Top left: Chocolate "snowballs" are just one of many treats you'll find on Germany's Romantic Road.
Top middle: Rothenburg is a medieval town known for its Christmas markets. *Top right:* A heart-shaped gingerbread Christmas cookie on display
Opposite: Look out at the onion-shaped rooftops of Augsburg Town Hall from the Perlach Tower

complete his castle circuit. You should also be sure to stop in the town of Füssen near the Austrian border before you head north. Set on a lake, bisected by a river, and still renowned for having produced the most sought-after handcrafted lutes, the town is the very picture of fairy-tale romance.

You could easily spend an eternity exploring what the Romantic Road holds in store, but if you don't have quite that much time, stick to a few highlights. Go to Pfaffenwinkel (Priests' Corner) for the pilgrimage churches (see **Play**); to Nördlingen and Dinkelsbühl for the medieval city walls; and to Rothenburg ob der Tauber for pretty much everything. One of the most celebrated stops on the entire Romantic Road, Rothenburg is Germany's best-preserved medieval town, with cobblestone streets, half-timber houses, imposing towers, and a particularly monumental local Christmas market. Dating back to the 15th century, Rothenburg's Advent festivities haven't changed much since then. In a medieval Marktplatz filled with local crafts, drinks, and sweets (don't miss the Rothenburg snowball, a schnapps-infused shortcrust pastry), you can still glimpse the Rothenburg Rider, the same character who's kicked off the Christmas season on horseback since the Middle Ages. Of course, to catch him, you'll have to time your visit to the start of Advent.

Continuing northward, you'll come upon more lovely Christmas markets: the one in the courtyard of the Renaissance-era Weikersheim Castle, for example, as well as the one outside Tauberbischofsheim's 13th-century Kurmainz Castle.

Finishing up, you'll find yourselves in the hilly, riverside town of Würzburg, right in the middle of a renowned wine region, where the only sensible thing to do is order up a bottle of the best local Bacchus and toast to your own fairy-tale ending.

Shoppers walk through Rothenburg's Christmas market, filled with food and gift stalls.

Opposite: Neuschwanstein Castle (New Swan Castle) *Above:* The frescoed ceilings of Parish Church of the Assumption of the Blessed Virgin Mary

PLAN YOUR TRIP

STAY • Hotel Tilman Riemenschneider, Rothenburg's half-timbered former brewery dating back to the 1500s (book the honey-moon rooms, which retain that old-timey feel with hand-painted four-poster beds). And the location can't be beat. If you had a glass too many of the white mulled wine (a local specialty) at the Christmas market, fret not: The Tilman is just a few minutes' walk away. *tilman-riemenschneider.de*

EAT • Bürgerspital Weinstuben, part of a 14th-century almshouse complex that now houses a winery, wine bar, and restaurant. Think vaulted ceilings, candlelit nooks, and award-winning house wines. Pair the famous dry-aged German beef with a glass of either Silvaner (white) or Blaufränkisch (red) wine. *buergerspital-weinstuben.de*

PLAY • Go to church. Christian or not,

you'll want to see the ancient local houses of worship in all their seasonal splendor. Perhaps the most famous on the Romantic Road are in the Pfaffenwinkel. Start with the Wieskirche, one of Germany's most important pilgrimage sites and rococo architecture examples. Then there's the 11th-century Rottenbuch Abbey, which was redone in baroque style in the 18th century and remains a parish church today.

SOUTHEAST ASIA

Where the Spiritual Meets the Sensual

Halong Bay in Vietnam turns gold and yellow at sunset.

In his celebrated essay "Why We Travel," Pico Iyer describes the aftermath of a trip to Southeast Asia: "I would lie in my bed, kept up by something more than jet lag . . . paging wistfully through my photographs and reading and re-reading my diaries, as if to extract some mystery from them. Anyone witnessing this strange scene would have drawn the right conclusion: I was in love." And Iyer's reaction to this magical world of rice terraces and temples is not at all uncommon. Somewhere between the floating markets and the karst isles—or the coconut milk and the lemongrass—you'll lose your heart, too.

Monks performing an alms ceremony in Luang Prabang

LUANG PRABANG, LAOS

An outsize jewel box at the mountainous confluence of the Mekong and Nam Khan Rivers, Luang Prabang is home to some of Buddhism's most opulent statement pieces. Explore the 16th-century Wat Xieng Thong, where thousands of prismatic tiles make up the floor-to-ceiling Tree of Life mosaic. But the filigreed facade of Wat Sene is also dazzling, as are the delicate golden spires of the hilltop Wat Chomsi, whose 328 steps lead to expansive river and city views.

And although you could spend your entire trip among the temples, you wouldn't want to miss some of the area's other draws—especially morning alms. This long-standing tradition is one of the world's best reasons to get up at 5 a.m., when laypeople line the streets to fill the local monks' begging bowls with sustenance. There's something so moving about these silent, saffron-robed men—and the reverent generosity they're met with—that you'll wish you could start every day this way. The best way to break the spell? With a cup of pungent coffee in one of the town's famed cafés, a holdover from the country's French colonial days.

PLAN YOUR TRIP

STAY Amantaka, where the sanctuary-like suites and tranquil gardens nod to Luang Prabang's Buddhist heritage, while posh furnishings nod to Laos's French colonial days. Many suites come with pools, but if you'd prefer to be on the river, book the resident boat for a private Mekong expedition, complete with onboard cocktails and an elegant meal. *aman.com*

The Taka Mekong Suite bedroom
at Amantaka in Luang Prabang

For the ultimate in romance, paddle through jade-colored secluded lagoons in Palawan's Bacuit Bay.

PALAWAN, PHILIPPINES

Despite recent media declarations to the contrary, Palawan isn't the world's most beautiful island. Or it's not *just* that, anyway. It's a whole province of islands—1,780 of them in total—each more exquisite than the last. Some are low-slung, curvaceous, and completely carpeted in virgin forest. Others are towering, jagged, and rock-faced, with spindly plants growing from their crevices at the most improbable angles. Still others are tiny fingers poking out of the surrounding emerald water—almost as if the Sulu and South China Seas, which share custody of the archipelago, were giving you a periodic thumbs-up.

And you can see why the universe would want to congratulate you for being here. Beyond the islands themselves, there are countless lagoons, caves, and coves to explore—ideally, by *bangka*. Half the fun of this traditional Filipino outrigger is never knowing what shade the bamboo floats will turn up in next. (Flamingo pink? Electric purple? Why not?)

But even the most flamboyant of floats are no match for the colors below the surface. Expect to swim, snorkel, or scuba dive among luminescent lavender anemones, Nemo-like clown fish, rainbow parrotfish, silver jackfish, yellow-striped sweetlips, and thousands of other underwater creatures.

One spot you shouldn't miss: the house reef at El Nido's Miniloc Island, a sister property to—and quick trip from—your own island digs (see **Stay**). Though you'll rightly feel loyal to your home turf of Lagen Island, the snorkeling at Miniloc will also inspire love at first sight—further evidence of every island's attempt to outdazzle all others here in Palawan.

PLAN YOUR TRIP

STAY El Nido Resorts' Lagen Island, which offers a crystalline cove for a welcome mat and forested limestone cliffs for a backyard. By day, a bangka will whisk you off to all the best local beaches and lagoons. By night, after the fabled Lagen Island sunset, the hotel can arrange a private dinner on the jetty—or a nearby sandbar. *elnidoresorts.com*

Make a point to visit the tiered rice paddies throughout Ubud in Bali.

BALI, INDONESIA

To see for yourselves why Bali was designated the "love" stop in Elizabeth Gilbert's mega best seller *Eat, Pray, Love,* head straight to Ubud, the misty, mountainous town where she lived—a favorite of Balinese royals as well. Home to emerald rice terraces, jungle-shrouded temples, and nighttime fire dances, Ubud is pure magic.

It also happens to be centrally located, so it's the perfect base for island-wide explorations. The rice terraces of Jatiluwih are a stunning starting point. Then hit the island's series of seaside temples—the most dramatic of which may well be the cliff-top, surf-pounded Pura Luhur Uluwatu, a prime sunset-spectating spot. And don't miss Mount Agung, the island's highest and holiest peak, where you'll find Bali's so-called Mother Temple of Besakih and appropriately astonishing views. To revive yourselves after all that climbing, take advantage of another famous Balinese offering: bliss-inducing Javanese treatments for two.

PLAN YOUR TRIP

STAY Como Shambhala, a series of secluded, luxuriously appointed villas scattered along a misty, sacred river valley. (Be warned: It's also home to monkeys that like to steal from your fruit basket.) The place is also renowned for its spa treatments, many offered in nature-shrouded open-air pavilions. *comohotels.com*

HAT KHAO LAK, THAILAND

An ancient trade corridor, the Andaman Sea has been plied by merchant vessels for millennia. But its coastline harbors riches infinitely greater than silk or spice: a whole series of the planet's most romantic beaches. Collectively known as Hat Khao Lak, these white, sandy stretches are backed by lushly forested hills, fronted by transparent turquoise water, and surrounded by countless dream possibilities.

The short list for your consideration: Take a traditional Thai longboat through the karst islands that punctuate the emerald waters of Phang Nga Bay. Or try an elephant trek and canoe safari through the jungles of Khao Sok National Park. You can also wander the markets and teahouses of the lovely local villages. But no matter where your explorations of Hat Khao Lak take you, some of your best memories will be of doing absolutely nothing, on one of those impossibly idyllic beaches.

PLAN YOUR TRIP

STAY The Sarojin, a lushly landscaped seaside spread with self-styled "imagineers" who create jaw-dropping private experiences. Among the many options is a starry swim and dinner for two at an entirely candlelit waterfall in a nearby jungle. Or Thai cooking classes for two by a river. Or an evening boat ride to the best local sunset view, where—naturally—champagne awaits. *sarojin.com*

Enjoy the privacy of curtained cabanas by the pool at the Sarojin resort in Thailand.

RIO DE JANEIRO

Sun, Sea, Sand and Samba

Even when it's not trying, Rio possesses a baseline sensuality that makes visitors swoon. Among the many who've observed the phenomenon, Barry White may have captured it best: "Any time, day or night, everything is so alive . . . it blows your mind." So imagine what Rio is like when it really turns up the heat during the famed Carnival festival every February: The combustible music. The sequin-spangled street parties. The free-flowing caipirinhas. The competitive kissing. All are set against one of the planet's most beautiful backdrops—a blend of rain forest, mountains, and beach. ❋ Of course, even if you don't

visit during Carnival, the legendary beaches will still be hopping. Remember: The North American winter is Brazil's summer, so you should plan to spend plenty of time swimming and, ahem, spectating at Ipanema, Copacabana, and Barra da Tijuca. Almost as dazzling? A walk on the iconic, wave-patterned tile sidewalk that borders the shore, with the requisite stops for fresh água de coco (coconut water) along the way. Also be sure to visit a beach that comes with a bonus: At the tiny Praia Vermelha, where the sand is reddish instead of the usual snow white, you can hop a cable car up to Sugarloaf Mountain for some of the most stunning, Rio-have-mercy views.

Top left: Sunset hits Ipanema Beach as surfers finish their day. *Top middle:* Visit during Carnival to participate in the lively festivities and look at the feathered and colorful costumes. *Top right:* The deluxe bedroom suite at the Fasano hotel

Take the cable car from Sugarloaf Mountain to Praia Vermelha, with a stop at Morro da Urca (722 feet up) in both directions.

PLAN YOUR TRIP

STAY • The Fasano, where you can be the girl (or guy) from Ipanema. Across the street from the legendary beach, this Philippe Starck–designed retreat evokes the golden age of bossa nova—one of the most storied and romantic eras in Rio's history—with vintage-inspired uniforms and midcentury-redux furniture. Book a room that overlooks the beach for views that are as good from bed as from your balcony. And to send you off to the sand in style, the hotel supplies flip-flops by designer Oskar Metsavaht. *fasano.com.br*

EAT • Aprazivel, a lushly landscaped hilltop collection of gazebos serving up views of downtown Rio and Guanabara Bay—and pan-Brazilian food with a twist (try the baked palm heart with pesto, basil, and cashews). By night, the toucan-filled garden becomes extra-magical, thanks to chandeliers and candles. *aprazivel.com.br*

PLAY • To get to the city's tallest peak—and visit the iconic Christ the Redeemer statue—take the slow road: the cog railway once used to ferry supplies up the Corcovado Mountain while the statue was in progress. Beyond experiencing a bit of history, you'll be passing through the stunning Tijuca Park, a massive urban forest. *tremdocorcovado.rio*

SWEDEN
JUKKASJÄRVI
Holiday on Ice

The aurora borealis lights up the sky in a Swedish forest near Kiruna.

Putting your relationship on ice is, well, the polar opposite of romantic. Except when you're *in* a polar region—specifically, Jukkasjärvi, where ice may well be the best thing that ever happened to you. You're here, naturally, to stay at the Icehotel, the only game in this one-street town of 550 residents, 124 miles north of the Arctic Circle. The world's first ice hotel, born in 1989 and reborn each winter, is a sprawling complex that won't disappoint. The whole experience is geared toward knocking a couple's (highly insulated) socks off—and it succeeds brilliantly. Emphasis on brilliant. Especially if you factor in the northern lights—as you should,

because winter is prime viewing time, and Jukkasjärvi is a prime viewing spot. There are no guarantees, but you can arrange attempted sightings of all kinds—from simply having the hotel wake you up in the event of a light show to taking a northern lights snowmobile tour to joining a sledborne "husky safari" with the region's most famous canines for drivers.

You can also take a side trip to the Aurora Sky Station in Abisco National Park, about 90 minutes away—arguably the best place on Earth to see the aurora, thanks to an almost perpetually cloudless sky. Even if you've already seen the northern lights, you may still want to visit the national park, where you'll don extra-warm "aurora-watchers' overalls," and

A small wooden church adds a shock of color to the stark white snow scene in Jukkasjärvi.

bundle up under blankets on the chairlift ride up to the sky station. At the top, you'll take in the darkest—and yet most brilliant—sky you can imagine. To move the romance needle right off the charts, book the four-course Nordic dinner—complete with reindeer steaks and local wine.

Of course, not all the action happens at night. By day, back in Jukkasjärvi, you can ride Icelandic horses into the local pine forest—a swath of wilderness that's frequently (and rightfully) compared to Narnia. Or you can cross-country ski, take an ice-sculpting class, or learn to photograph the glorious, but technically difficult, night skies. You can also explore the indigenous Sami community, whether at a museum or on a traditional reindeer sled.

Not that you should ignore Jukkasjärvi itself. The main drag makes for a lovely, if brief, walk. The only official stop on this self-guided tour? The 17th-century wooden Sami church, Lapland's oldest surviving house of worship, complete with a birch and reindeer horn organ.

If the church starts to give you ideas, remember that there's another one you may want to hold out for: the hotel's improbably cozy Ice Church, where you can orchestrate a most dazzling proposal, vow renewal, or—if you've come prepared—wedding.

Whatever adventures you choose on this trip—whether you're outdoors under the night sky or indoors on your fancy ice block of a bed—you will grow closer in the process,

Exchange vows in front of the Icehotel's igloo.

largely by necessity. Seriously: You'll never snuggle more than you will here. And you'll never be so wowed by just chilling—together.

PLAN YOUR TRIP

STAY • Icehotel, where you can choose between "cool" rooms (made of ice) and warm rooms (conventional and not made of ice)—or ideally, a combination thereof. (The truth is, most people find that one night on ice is enough.) No two cool rooms are exactly alike. They range from simple snow or ice rooms with animal skin–draped ice beds to massive deluxe art suites with pillow-top mattresses and private changing rooms. And some feature the biggest luxury of all (at least in the world of ice hotels): en suite bathrooms and saunas. *icehotel.com*

EAT • The Wilderness Dinner, located at the Icehotel's satellite wilderness camp. After welcome drinks and a multicourse feast in a cabin, you'll stretch out on reindeer skins to stare at the star-studded (and probably aurora-illuminated) polar sky. Next come dessert, coffee, and a ride home to your ice castle.

PLAY • Sauna like Swedes on the grounds of the hotel. There's a 10-part ritual that includes a plunge into the river that produces the ice hotel's building blocks, and—less bracing—a soak in a wood-fired outdoor bath.

UNIQUE LODGES
OF THE WORLD

Find more inspired retreats with National Geographic Unique Lodges of the World, a hand-picked collection that offers guests an intimate encounter with some of the planet's most treasured places. From stunning safari tents to private thatched bungalows in the rain forest, these lodges provide an extraordinary guest experience while protecting the habitats and cultures that surround them. Visit *natgeolodges.com* to book a romantic getaway that is truly rich and meaningful at one of these incredible locations:

* AFRICA *

**GROOTBOS PRIVATE
NATURE RESERVE**
Western Cape, South Africa

KASBAH DU TOUBKAL
High Atlas Mountains, Morocco

MARA PLAINS CAMP
Olare Motorogi
Conservancy, Kenya

OL DONYO LODGE
Chyulu Hills, Kenya

RUBONDO ISLAND CAMP
Rubondo Island National Park,
Tanzania

SABI SABI EARTH LODGE
Sabi Sand Reserve, South Africa

SAYARI CAMP
Serengeti National Park, Tanzania

THE BUSHCAMP COMPANY
South Luangwa National Park, Zambia

TSWALU KALAHARI
Kalahari, South Africa

ZARAFA CAMP
Selinda Reserve, Botswana

FREGATE ISLAND PRIVATE
Fregate Island, The Seychelles

**BUSHMANS KLOOF WILDERNESS
RESERVE & WELLNESS RETREAT**
Western Cape, South Africa

SEGERA RETREAT
Laikipia Plateau, Kenya

SARARA CAMP
Namunyak Wildlife Conservancy,
South Africa

* ASIA *

SUKAU RAINFOREST LODGE
Sabah, Malaysian Borneo

THREE CAMEL LODGE
Gobi, Mongolia

ZHIWA LING HOTEL
Paro, Bhutan

BANYAN TREE RINGHA
Shangri-La, China

* AUSTRALIA *
AND THE PACIFIC

CAPELLA LODGE
Lord Howe Island,
Australia

LIZARD ISLAND
Great Barrier Reef,
Australia

LONGITUDE 131°
The Northern Territory,
Australia

SOUTHERN OCEAN LODGE
Kangaroo Island,
Australia

THE BRANDO
Tetiaroa, French Polynesia

CENTRAL AMERICA AND THE CARIBBEAN

PETIT ST. VINCENT PRIVATE ISLAND RESORT
Petit St. Vincent, St. Vincent and the Grenadines

PACUARE LODGE
Limón Province, Costa Rica

ROSALIE BAY RESORT
Morne Trois Pitons, Dominica

LAPA RIOS ECO LODGE
Osa Peninsula, Costa Rica

TIAMO RESORT
South Andros Island, Bahamas

EUROPE

KAPARI NATURAL RESORT
Santorini, Greece

ARISTI MOUNTAIN RESORT & VILLAS
Aristi, Greece

ASHFORD CASTLE
Mayo, Ireland

NORTH AMERICA

CUIXMALA
Costalegre, Mexico

FOGO ISLAND INN
Newfoundland, Canada

HACIENDA DE SAN ANTONIO
Colima, Mexico

NIMMO BAY WILDERNESS RESORT
British Columbia, Canada

LONE MOUNTAIN RANCH
Big Sky, Montana, United States

SIWASH LAKE WILDERNESS RESORT
British Columbia, Canada

THE RANCH AT ROCK CREEK
Western Montana Wilderness, United States

TUTKA BAY LODGE
Kenai Peninsula, Alaska, United States

WINTERLAKE LODGE
South-Central Alaskan Wilderness, United States

CHURCHILL WILD–SEAL RIVER HERITAGE LODGE
Manitoba, Canada

THE BENTWOOD INN
Jackson Hole, Wyoming, United Statesmi

SOUTH AMERICA

INKATERRA HACIENDA CONCEPCIÓN
Amazon Rain Forest, Peru

INKATERRA HACIENDA URUBAMBA
Sacred Valley of the Inca, Peru

INKATERRA LA CASONA
Cusco, Peru

INKATERRA MACHU PICCHU PUEBLO HOTEL
Machu Picchu Pueblo, Peru

MASHPI LODGE
Chocó Rain Forest, Ecuador

TIERRA ATACAMA HOTEL & SPA
Atacama Desert, Chile

TIERRA PATAGONIA HOTEL & SPA
Patagonia, Chile

RESERVA DO IBITIPOCA
Minas Gerais, Brazil

Southern Ocean Lodge in Kangaroo Island, Australia

ABOUT THE AUTHOR

Abbie Kozolchyk is an award-winning writer and editor specializing in travel. She has contributed to *Travel + Leisure, National Geographic Traveler, Forbes Traveler, Condé Nast Traveler, World Hum,* and the Best Women's Travel Writing anthology series.

ACKNOWLEDGMENTS

Book writing—though perhaps most efficient as a solitary pursuit—is much more enjoyable as a group activity. At least in my experience. Happily, I have an embarrassment of wordsmiths in my life, several of whom read and significantly improved these pages. Topping the list is my mother, Billie Kozolchyk, who—despite being predisposed to love whatever her children do—*will* occasionally note a lackluster adjective. Then there's my love, Jim Benning, who—in addition to being an exquisite human being—has rightly been called the best editor west of the Mississippi (by people far less biased than I). Next comes Catalan Conlon, my friend since birth, who not only read everything for clarity but helped with the research as well. To say nothing of my friend Lavinia Spalding, editor of a stack of brilliant travel anthologies—and master of the tweak that makes everything better. And finally, my friend Allyson Dickman, of whom I was already in awe when we worked together at Rachael Ray's magazine—and whose ability to save the day (editorially and otherwise) has only increased since she became a National Geographic Books editor. *My* editor, in fact.

Speaking of National Geographic Books people, I owe a huge debt of gratitude to the one who dreamed up this book in the first place and worked tirelessly on its execution: deputy editor Hilary Black. And to art director Elisa Gibson and photo editors Moira Haney and Krista Rossow for making each page so gorgeous.

Then there are the people who created my roving writer's retreat. Huge thanks to my godsons Benjamin and Jacob Kaye, who not only forfeited their playroom so I could sleep and write in it but urged me on with hourly checks of my progress. And to Rachael and Sammie Cooper, who patiently brainstormed with me as my colony of research materials spread ever farther across their house. And to Mbuso Mbata, a front desk clerk at the Hilton Durban, who—when I showed up in desperate need of nothing more than an Internet connection that would let me finish and file a chapter—installed me in the best room he had, simply because he loves books and thought I could use some inspiration.

Inspired I was—as much by the kindness of strangers as by the surroundings. But the kindness of *friends* has been truly epic. With that in mind, I offer infinite thanks to, in no particular order, Cheryl, David, Farley, Gady, Assaf, Julie, Jeff, Sammy, Scott, Ruby, Max, Pia, Marc, Luca, Noah, Andrew, Kirsten, Maria, Sally, David, Ilan, Hannah, Maya, Josh, Ronnie, Tammy, Reyna, Abie, Batsheva, Manu, Debbie, Sammy, Sonia, Abram, Ross, Rachel, Jenna, Elianna, Alison, Courtney, Jessie, Karen, Joel, Phoebe, Abs, Rich, Ellie, Nathan, Lisa, Tim, Linda, Alyse, Vic, Edan, Tal, Ayelet, Cliff, Jordan, Eytan, Layla, Laura, Nancy, Shana, Luis, Mari, Sofi, Eva, Mateo, Richard, Ralf, JD, Karen, Dan, Tom, Matt, Anat, Jenna, Jeryl, Suzanne, Barbara, Suzanne, Joe, Masha, Adam, Alan, Emma, Erin, Sean, Frank, Leyla, Lolita, Sue, Joyce, Marie Laure, Arabella, Anja, Sandra, Jill, Kylie, the Rachael Ray team, and the entire sisterhood of beauty editors.

But most of all, I thank my family: my spectacularly devoted, supportive, and kvelling parents, Billie and Boris, who instilled a love of the world and its inhabitants in me from birth (and probably even before that, given that I was traveling around Central America for most of my time in utero); my *tía* Marta, who shows up for everything and everyone; and my sister, Shaunie, my brother-in-law, David, my brother, Raphael, and my sister-in-law, Diana, who've given me the most unqualifiedly delicious source of inspiration in my life: Sigal, Liana, Ethan, Alex, and Jacob.

ILLUSTRATIONS CREDITS

Redux; 128 (LE), Richard Cummins/Getty Images; 128 (CTR), Cultura RM Exclusive/Matt Dutile/Getty Images; 128 (RT), dask side of pink/Shutterstock; 129, Wolfgang Kaehler/Getty Images; 130-31, Andreas Hub/laif/Redux; 132, Oliver Hoffmann/Getty Images; 133, Franz Marc Frei/LOOK-foto/Getty Images; 134 (LE), John W Banagan/Getty Images; 134 (CTR), Courtesy of Banyan Tree Hotels and Resorts; 134 (RT), toiletroom/Shutterstock; 135, Simon Montgomery/robertharding/Getty Images; 136-7, f11photo/Shutterstock; 138, Courtesy of Banyan Tree Hotels and Resorts; 139, Courtesy of Banyan Tree Hotels and Resorts; 140-41, Fesus Robert Levente/Getty Images; 142 (LE), Fuse/Getty Images; 142 (CTR), Baloncici/Getty Images; 142 (RT) Baloncici/Getty Images; 143, Grant Faint/Getty Images; 144-5, Aurora Photos/Alamy Stock Photo; 146, Kodiak Greenwood, courtesy of Post Ranch Inn; 147, Aurora Photos/Alamy Stock Photo; 148 (LE), Michael Melford/National Geographic Creative; 148 (CTR), Modrow/laif/Redux; 148 (RT), Bartosz Hadyniak/Getty Images; 149, Roberto A. Sanchez/Getty Images; 150-51, Jan Skwara/Getty Images; 152, scorpp/Getty Images; 153, Courtesy of Taj Hotels Resorts and Palaces; 154-5, Reynold Mainse/Design Pics/Getty Image; 156, Courtesy of Isrotel Hotel Chain; 157, FedevPhoto/Getty Images; 158 (LE), Krista Rossow; 158 (CTR), Krista Rossow; 158 (RT), Clay McLachlan/Getty Images; 159, Krista Rossow; 160-61, Huber/Sime/eStock Photo; 162, Krista Rossow; 163, Andrew Bain/Getty Images; 164-5, Lucas Vallecillos/VWPics/Redux; 166, Courtesy of Four Seasons Hotel Prague; 167, Jan Sagl/Anzenberger/Redux; 168-9, gehringj/Getty Images; 170, Tim E White/

Getty Images; 171, SIME/eStock Photo; 172-3, Courtesy of Castello di Casole—A Timbers Resort; 174, sorincolac/Getty Images; 175, Sofie Delauw/Getty Images; 176 (LE), Courtesy of COMO Hotels and Resorts; 176 (CTR), narvikk/Getty Images; 176 (RT), Ira Block/National Geographic Creative; 177, Wes Walker/Getty Images; 178-9, Courtesy of COMO Hotels and Resorts; 180, narvikk/Getty Images; 181, narvikk/Getty Images; 182-3, Peter Zelei Images/Getty Images; 184, Cortyn/Shutterstock; 185, Jonathan Smith/Getty Images; 186 (LE), Izabela Habur/Getty Images; 186 (CTR), Courtesy of Inkaterra Hotels; 186 (RT), Bartosz Hadyniak/Getty Images; 187, traveler1116/Getty Images; 188-9, Cultura RM Exclusive/Philip Lee Harvey/Getty Images; 190, YinYang/Getty Images; 191, Courtesy of Inkaterra Hotels; 192 (LE), Rudy Balasko/Shutterstock; 192 (CTR), James T. Murray/Courtesy of Gramercy Park Hotel; 192 (RT), Steve Prezant/Getty Images; 193, espiegle/Getty Images; 194-5, SIME/eStock Photo; 196, Jason Loucas/Qualia Resorts; 197, Emmanuel Valentin/Getty Images; 198-9, Courtesy of Badrutt's Palace Hotel; 200-201, Jeffrey B. Banke/Shutterstock; 202, Wild-Places/Getty Images; 203, Courtesy of Blanket Bay; 204 (LE), Palani Mohan/Getty Images; 204 (CTR), ferrantraite/Getty Images; 204 (RT), Palani Mohan/Getty Images; 205, Peter Adams/Getty Images; 206-207, Michelle Chaplow, courtesy of Oberoi Hotels & Resorts; 208, Nikada/Getty Images; 209, Photo by Prasit Chansareekorn/Getty Images; 210 (LE), Courtesy of Badrutt's Palace Hotel; 210 (CTR), Courtesy of Badrutt's Palace Hotel; 210 (RT), Prisma Bildagentur AG/Alamy Stock Photo; 211, Alessandro Colle/Shutterstock; 212 (LE), BlueOrange Studio/

Shutterstock; 212 (CTR), Paul Sutherland/National Geographic Creative; 212 (RT), AWL Images/Getty Images; 213, Courtesy of Jumeirah Hotels & Resorts; 214-15, brandtbolding/Getty Images; 216, BorisVetshev/Shutterstock; 217, Tony Anderson/Getty Images; 218-19, windjunkie/Getty Images; 220, Courtesy of Fairmont Hotels & Resorts; 221, Courtesy of Fairmont Hotels & Resorts; 222-3, Courtesy of Cheval Blanc; 224, Richard I'Anson/Getty Images; 225, Courtesy of Cheval Blanc; 226-7, Courtesy of Jade Mountain; 228, Cultura RM Exclusive/Russ Rohde/Getty Images; 229, Nature Picture Library/Alamy Stock Photo; 230 (LE), Eurasia Press/Getty Images; 230 (CTR), Martin Froyda/Shutterstock; 230 (RT), Juergen Sack/Getty Images; 231, Michael Thaler/Shutterstock; 232-3, Mark Titterton/Alamy Stock Photo; 234, Achim Thomae/Getty Images; 235, imageBROKER/Alamy Stock Photo; 236-7, sergwsqr/Getty Images; 238, Ignazio Sciacca/laif/Redux; 239, Courtesy of Aman; 240-41, Mon Corpuz Photography/Getty Images; 242, Kevin Miller/Getty Images; 243, Courtesy of The Sarojin; 244 (LE), luoman/Getty Images; 244 (CTR), Buda Mendes/Getty Images; 244 (RT), Courtesy of Hotel Fasano Rio de Janeiro; 245, Nikada/Getty Images; 246-7, Dave Moorhouse/Getty Images; 248, Ragnar Th. Sigurdsson/Getty Images; 249, Asaf Kliger/www.icehotel.com; 251, Courtesy of Southern Ocean Lodge/National Geographic Unique Lodge of the World.

THE WORLD'S MOST
ROMANTIC
DESTINATIONS

Since 1888, the National Geographic Society has funded more than 12,000 research, exploration, and preservation projects around the world. National Geographic Partners distributes a portion of the funds it receives from your purchase to National Geographic Society to support programs including the conservation of animals and their habitats.

National Geographic Partners
1145 17th Street NW
Washington, DC 20036-4688 USA

Become a member of National Geographic and activate your benefits today at natgeo.com/jointoday.

For information about special discounts for bulk purchases, please contact National Geographic Books Special Sales: specialsales@natgeo.com

For rights or permissions inquiries, please contact National Geographic Books Subsidiary Rights: bookrights@natgeo.com

ISBN: 978-1-4262-1706-7

Printed in Hong Kong

16/THK/1

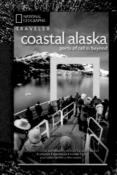